AGENCE MICHELLE LAPAUTRE

6, rue Jean Carriès - 75007 Paris

Tél. : 01 47 34 82 41   Fax : 01 47 34 00 90

INTO THE DARKNESS LAUGHING

INTO THE DARKNESS LAUGHING

The Story of Modigliani's Last Mistress, Jeanne Hébuterne

PATRICE CHAPLIN

VIRAGO

By the same author

Having it Away
The Unforgotten
Siesta
Harriet Hunter
Don Salino's Wife
Albany Park
Another City
By Flower and Dean Street
The Fame People
Forget Me Not

Published by VIRAGO PRESS Limited 1990
20–23 Mandela Street, Camden Town, London NW1 0HQ

Copyright © Patrice Chaplin 1990

*A CIP catalogue record for this book
is available from the British Library*

Typeset by CentraCet, Cambridge
Printed in Great Britain by
Bookcraft (Bath) Ltd.

Acknowledgements and Sources

I am indebted to the following publications: Jeanne Modigliani, *Modigliani sans légende*, Paris, 1961; Douglas Goldring, *Artists' Quarter*, London, 1941; *Recollections of Modigliani by Those Who Knew Him*, Los Angeles, 1958; Nina Hamnett, *Laughing Torso*, London, 1932; Ambrogio Ceroni, *Amedeo Modigliani*, Milan, 1958; André Salmon, *La Vie passionnée de Modigliani*; Pierre Sichel, *Modigliani*, London, 1967; and to the following people: Frédérique Prud'hon, Georges Charaire, Madame Schalit, Victor Nechtschein-Leduc, Marika Rivera, Ulla Fribrock, Louise Cornou, Charlotte Trench, Aimée Soutine, Monsieur Percival.

LIST OF ILLUSTRATIONS

Work by Jeanne Hébuterne on pages ii, 1, 33, 37, 60, 87, 120, 137, 149 is reproduced by kind permission of Madame Frédérique Prud'hon, photographs by Percival.

My parents Germaine Labaye and Roger Wild, taking part in Montparnasse life, of course met Jeanne Hébuterne and Amedeo Modigliani before the twenties. And my mother became an intimate friend to Jeanne H. But that friendship I quite ignored till the couple's daughter, Jeanne Modigliani, asked my parents about her own.

After my father's death, in September 1987, Laurent, my eldest son, and I found among family papers a small locked metal casket in which my mother had hidden the precious letters sent her by Jeanne Hébuterne in her happy time. The very memory of that past, so aching – Jeanne's story and dramatic death, was the secret my mother could not share. But I believe it puts salve on those wounds finally to open the casket and understand Jeanne.

Frédérique PRUD'HON

Prelude

J. Kibstrom

On 22 September 1987 I was sitting in the local hospital waiting-room. All around me were pregnant women. The room was very hot and as I waited, I turned the pages of an old magazine. I noticed a small reproduction of a Modigliani painting recently sold at Sotheby's, and underneath it a short description of the painter and his last mistress, Jeanne Hébuterne.

The scrap of story made me turn icy cold because I felt that it was already known to me. Something from the past, it was not unfamiliar. And it should have been. I knew nothing whatsoever about Modigliani. I didn't even know he was Italian. I knew only his style of painting. I left the waiting-room without even hearing the results of the scan.

At first I wondered if it was the part of me that wrote that was aroused. The story? It was mine. I felt totally possessive about these two doomed lovers. I immediately tried to get information about Modigliani and Jeanne Hébuterne.

Before I got the books or read one word I decided to take a holiday. It was November. I wanted to go to the place I always returned to – Gerona in Spain. My friend Stewart said he'd come with me. Unaccountably, I suddenly wanted to arrive in Gerona from a new direction. Instead of flying to Barcelona and taking the train north, I wanted to approach the city from France: a train perhaps from Marseille or Perpignan. I had no explanation for this desire and supposed it was an attempt to liven up a well-trod route to a place I knew too well. I decided the most pleasant place to go from would be Nice. I now very much wanted to visit that part of the Mediterranean where I'd never been before. But every time Stewart and I booked a hotel or a plane, something stopped the journey. An air traffic control strike, then Air France went on strike, no seats on other planes, hotels overbooked, then other commitments came along. I made about ten attempts to get to Nice, a place I had hardly given a thought to before. In the end we went to Folkestone.

When I did start the research I found that Modigliani and Jeanne had gone to Nice. They'd taken the train from Paris in March 1918 to get away from the war, to try and improve Modigliani's health. She was just pregnant with their first child. They stayed over a year.

I supposed that my sudden irrational desire to go to Nice was coincidental, but when I read the biographies I saw many connections with my own life. More than coincidences, they were familiar. And they were linked to José, my Spanish love whom I'd met when, at fifteen, I'd first gone to Gerona. I could see him so clearly as I read about Modigliani. It would be ludicrous for me to say that my relationship with José had been a success, but it had dominated my life, and had been the subject of more than one book. And when I'd first seen him we, too, were not unknown to each other. We both felt: yes, all right, we meet again – for good or ill. At the time I mistook this recognition for love. José viewed it differently. For a Spaniard to meet someone they thought they'd known in a previous life was a fearful event. They treated the person as a ghost, turned away and said their prayers.

Remembering my life with José stirred other older memories and included Paris, which never suited either of us. We could never get our lives right in that city, and it had peculiar reverberations. I remember in the late sixties going into a restaurant in Les Halles run by two retired actresses. It still retained its former style – thirties? Earlier? And we both felt, but didn't say until later, that entering that restaurant was completely familiar. It was as though we'd been there just a minute before. Paris was such a malevolent city when it came to our relationship – worse than any deceived and jealous husband or wife. On our first visit, we'd arrived from Spain by the night train intending to get married. He was twenty-four and I was sixteen. We'd quarrelled before we'd even left the station. Coincidentally, we'd arrived on the anniversary of Modigliani's death, 24 January.

As I read about Modigliani's life, all the horror and pain I'd experienced in that city came back. I was fifteen when I first stepped on to its boulevards. It was as though I'd already suffered there. It wasn't a fresh city. In supposing that I was discovering the 'new' I was being duped. I might not realise I knew the city, but it knew me. That's how I saw it now. In that place I could never win. I could go in like a movie star and be reduced to a beggar in one short hour. Yet for years I hadn't properly accepted it. I'd still keep passing through on the way to somewhere else, determined to feel all right. After all, it was just another city. But after what I could only term as spiteful ill luck on my last visit, four years ago, I had decided never to go back. The place was bigger than me, didn't suit me. I'd simply go to places that did.

So it was with some reluctance that I decided to return – but how else would I find out about their lives, except by being there? My French agent said, 'It's all been written. What else is there to say?' I didn't know. I knew only that I had to speak to people who remembered something about their lives and find out why they were doomed.

Not one biographer describing the painter Amedeo Modigliani's life has given a fair account of Jeanne Hébuterne, his friend and last mistress. The early source material was provided by friends and acquaintances who were deeply shocked and in some cases felt guilty about Modigliani's despairing death and Jeanne's suicide. Many of those closest to them refused to speak at all. The first biographers cast her as a madonna, beyond reproach. They never gave her any lines to speak because they didn't have any.

André Salmon, in his biography *La Vie passionnée de Modigliani*, manages to give him at least a satisfactorily passionate love affair, writing Jeanne up in a suitable way for that purpose. But he was also thinking of the feelings of Jeanne's family and the orphaned daughter, Jeanne Modigliani. He decided that only the sweetest light should fall on the doomed mother. The daughter, in fact, was irritated by the legends surrounding her parents and tried tracking down and talking to surviving friends, acquaintances and rivals to get a truthful picture. She established that her mother was not the weak submissive creature, half-victim, half-madonna, presented by the early writers; she had a strong character, original powers of thought, and a decided talent as an artist.

Reading her book *Modigliani sans légende*, I felt that she had been fobbed off. People would not necessarily tell her the truth. She was the orphan of this tragedy. Modigliani had chosen to die like a dog in the artists' community, not with his family. The artists guarded him as their own. The family were outsiders and would be placated with careful and soothing stories.

Before he died he was a barely recognised painter, considered a quarrelsome drunk with self-destructive habits. And the Catholic Jeanne, from a bourgeois French family, was considered ill advised in her attachment to him. They'd spent several days – André Salmon and the painter Ortiz de Zárate said as much as a whole week – totally alone in the studio, with no heating and only tins of sardines to eat and bottles of wine and marc to drink. He was dying; she was about to give birth to their second child. Yet she didn't get help for herself or for him. This was never challenged in the biographies. It certainly worried me. To get help for the dying is an instinctive act, and she herself needed care. What terrible event had happened to paralyse her so totally? According to Salmon and Ortiz de Zárate, Modigliani's friends had all deserted the couple. The sculptor Indenbaum said the same. Yet after his death and her suicide, the victims were recast as 'genius' and 'sacrificial lamb'. Jeanne had sacrificed her art and life for him. The legends began; prices for Modigliani's pictures soared. The dealers haggled at the funeral ceremony. The friends who had been absent in the last days now rewrote their lives, putting themselves in the picture. Nobody wanted to seem to have turned their back on genius.

Amedeo Modigliani was a middle-class Italian Sephardic Jew who left Livorno in 1906, when he was twenty-two, to find success in Paris, art capital of the world. But he was not a man of his time. He did not fit into the Montmartre of Picasso and his acolytes at the Bateau-Lavoir, or the Futurists with their rebellious manifesto. In a dark world of hashish pellets, drink and the impoverished characters of the Maquis, he remained aloof. He felt at home with the outsiders, Utrillo and later Soutine. Everyone who has recorded their impressions of him emphasises his charisma and mesmerising powers. He was fatally attractive to women, and to many men. He knew he was doomed and predicted 'a short but intense life'. Unable to gain recognition for his work, he endured poverty, addiction, illness, despair. He died of tubercular meningitis in a Charity hospital aged thirty-five. He was the last great Bohemian and the subject of much speculation.

Little, however, was known of Jeanne. The early romantic picture became the established one, well documented in Pierre Sichel's *Modigliani*, written in 1967. Fifield changed all that in 1973. In his biography he made assumptions about what the artist liked and disliked, one of his dislikes being Jeanne Hébuterne, whom Fifield described as 'common'. He painted his own very definite character portrait of Jeanne, concluding that she was disastrous for Modigliani, and from this denigration of Jeanne arose the latest biographies in which Fifield's hypothetical statements are taken as fact. After all, who would challenge him? Certainly not Jeanne's brother André, still alive in his nineties, or his wife Georgette, ten years younger. They had maintained a policy of silence. Jeanne's closest friends also remained silent. So did their children. Modigliani's family did not know Jeanne. When the daughter died in 1984, the witnesses from 1920 could have cast off restraint and told a truth less polite, but most of them are now also dead.

As I read the biographies I became increasingly dismayed because each writer constantly contradicted himself on the subject of Jeanne – except the last, who were positively against her. And too many questions were left not only unanswered but unchallenged. The early writers wallowed in supposition and produced fictionalised accounts of how things could have been in the light of how they'd chosen to see her. It was unconvincing because Modigliani would not have gone for the girl they described. He may have been wrecked, drunk, bitter and ill, but he still had his original vision and perception unimpaired, as is evident in his last paintings. He had a decided taste. This creation of the biographers would not have lasted a week. And he would hardly have produced at least twenty-four portraits of this woman, together with countless drawings, if she had been such an irritant.

In January 1988 I was fortunate to find, in Paris, Victor Nechtstein-Leduc, the widower of Modigliani's daughter Jeanne. She too had been a painter. The flat was immense, once elegant. Although it was nearly February, a Christmas tree had not been removed from the living-room. It was lopsided and sparsely decorated with tinsel, now dusty. I was accompanied by my assistant, Jacqueline, who had spent an aeon of time doing herself up. All wasted in here. The widower was small, bald and cautious.

I took out a tape-recorder and said, 'Do you mind? Will this disturb you?'

He replied, 'It won't disturb me at all because I have nothing to say.' He said it with a certain pride.

I looked at Jacqueline, disbelieving. She had set up the meeting. All this effort, tension and expense to arrive in the enemy city for nothing.

'But on the telephone you said you had something to say,' I told him.

'I can't say anything about my wife's parents because she had never known them. She was fourteen months old when they died.'

'But people must have told her stories, given her information over the years.'

He didn't think she was curious. This turned out to be untrue. Later I found out that Jeanne Modigliani had searched Paris for her father's and mother's friends, to find information.

The widower said she was brought up by Modigliani's sister Margherita in Italy. He said he'd met her in Toulouse during the German Occupation. They were both working for the Resistance. Back in Paris they'd got married and had two daughters, one handicapped. I understood that his wife's last years had been very unhappy. He indicated that she drank, and had finally lost her mind. They'd divorced in 1980 and she'd died in 1984.

He showed us into another room; it could be described as disordered. On the walls, amongst childish drawings and the ones by his deceased wife, were paintings and drawings by Jeanne Hébuterne, including her painting of a tree in a courtyard. And there were drawings by Modigliani. Jacqueline nearly passed out. 'In this squalor you find these. He does not know what he has.'

I was back in London. In the William Fifield biography there was a reproduction of the artists of Montparnasse with Modigliani in the centre, by Marevna, a Russian artist. And I recalled that when the proposed wedding to José had fallen apart in the Paris station, I'd returned, after a certain hellish interval, to London and gone almost immediately to stay for a few days in the house of Marika, a music-hall artist and actress, daughter of Marevna and the primitive, powerful Mexican painter Diego Rivera. I had no idea if Marika was in London, if she'd remember me. A lot of time had passed – I hadn't seen her and Marevna for possibly twenty-five years. I wanted to talk to her. I was almost sure Marevna had died, but felt certain Marika would know something about Modigliani.

With difficulty I found her address. She lived in the same house I had visited. I now saw that research was not unlike detective work. She remembered me, and I her. Some people never really change. She was still charged with life and exotic glamour, quite ageless.

What Marika knew about Modigliani had come from Marevna, who had modelled for him. He was also, for a while, friendly with Diego Rivera, the love of Marevna's life. Marevna had been present when Modigliani had thrown his lover Beatrice Hastings through a window without opening it first. She'd described him entering a room: he brought such warmth and radiance. It made me think of José, of the way he used to be, the way I'd described him in my book *Albany Park*. 'Of course he was ...' Marika stopped. Why should she tell me everything – or anything? She held the memories of Modigliani to her, like treasure. And I understood it was not just memory but her life, her mother's life. Many people took that attitude towards Modigliani, keeping him for themselves, whereas Picasso they'd talk about quite openly. But then Picasso was common currency. He didn't have the same physical presence or mystery. Modigliani brought an extra heightened quality into the lives of those he loved, and many were left out, jealous. Soutine adored Modigliani because he was everything the Russian could never be. Also, he was generous and the first to discover and promote Soutine's talent. It was Modigliani who insisted that the dealer Zborowski should take him on. I asked Marika about Modigliani's life with Jeanne.

'*Chérie*, all the women adored him.'

'And Jeanne?'

'He was sweet and tender to her, but he had that Englishwoman Hastings under his skin.'

9

For some reason I didn't want to hear that. I wanted him to love Jeanne. 'What was Jeanne like?'

'Very silent, adoring, his friend until death, his only friend. Her talent was put aside. She gave everything to him. She was the sacrificial lamb. He was so loved by the artists that his funeral was fantastic, like that of a prince. All of Montparnasse was there. Whereas Jeanne was buried discreetly in the suburbs.'

I found that whoever I spoke to about Modigliani had decided views for or against. Because he was a legend and women liked to be linked to his life, it seemed that everyone had slept with him. I found that hard to believe, seeing the amount of drink and drugs he used. If he did it as much as they said he did, then he was a medical miracle. I am sure there were as many sick days as sexual ones.

Marika explained that poverty was not unusual in Montparnasse. Drink and drugs were in common use. It was quite accepted amongst the artists that everyone slept with everyone else. 'Maman said that when a baby was born everyone looked over the cradle to see who was the father.'

The Polish actor Vladyk Sheybal told me how Marevna, for a time, would receive a visit from Modigliani every day. He'd always bring her a rose. She knew he had no money to buy flowers and finally asked where he was getting the roses. He said, 'On my way to you I pass a church. There's always someone being buried there. I take a flower off the coffin. I have more need of it than a corpse!'

One day my friend Geoff Sharpe, a film designer, rang and said, 'I just saw a friend of mine who's married to a French girl and I mentioned what you were doing. She has a sister who is going out with the grandson of a painter who knew Modigliani, Roger Wild. And his wife was Jeanne Hébuterne's best friend, Germaine Labaye. They've left letters and photographs. You should phone their daughter, Madame Prud'hon. She'll be able to talk to you about that time.'

Geoff came with me to Paris because the chance finding of Madame Prud'hon excited him. At Charles de Gaulle airport I had a quick meal before going to see her in the elegant suburbs because I had a

10

great respect for the variety of harm Paris can do me. I wanted to give myself the best chance to win. A sugar crisis in the suburbs could be a bad thing and I was becoming aware that the French are not over-hospitable if they don't know you.

Madame Prud'hon was energetic and good-looking. We sat together in a soothing room with blue and silver ornaments. I didn't really look at the surroundings as I was trying to cram a lot in before she went off for her holiday at five o'clock. The table was covered with letters and photographs but she controlled the interview, reading me sentences her father had written on the Jeanne Hébuterne affair. André Salmon, before writing his book in the fifties, had written to Roger Wild trying to re-establish facts about the Modigliani–Jeanne relationship. Roger Wild had written back. Madame Prud'hon had his letter. André Salmon had wanted memories of that time, but her father had felt too distressed by the tragedy. Her mother rarely spoke of it. It was an appalling affair that shocked everyone. I felt now that I was intruding upon a personal grief and changed the subject. What was Modigliani like?

'Passionate, fascinating. Nothing like in the movie *Montparnasse 19*.'

'Did she love him?'

'If she hadn't loved him she wouldn't have thrown herself from the window.'

I felt there were many reasons for killing oneself other than lost love. Madame Prud'hon shuddered, remembering something private her mother had told her.

When it was dark, Geoff and I went up the rue Lepic to the place du Tertre, which was full of tourists as usual. Lower down and off to the side of the rue Norvins, where Modigliani had lived with the writer Beatrice Hastings, I found a peaceful place with trees and a bench; from here I could look over Paris. It was called the place Calvaire. The air was fresh and the trees were already in bloom. Below, steep steps, at least fifty, were lit by old-fashioned lamps. The central iron rail was original and engraved with ivy leaves and the lamp stems were also decorated, dating from the early part of the century, perhaps before. He would have held that rail as he came up from the Pigalle bars. He would have rested at the top, where I now sat, before continuing to his temporary address in the place du Tertre or the Maquis.

I could see right across Paris to the fields beyond. This view would have been the same: the Eiffel Tower already there, fewer lights, more fields. I held the cold stair-rail and imagined the lamps in those days, lit by gas, throwing a pool of light which moved in the wind. Below, the same streets with the same cobblestones, washing hanging out across the road, low iron balconies, sunshine. I leant over the stone wall and looked at the shuttered windows. Only the paint would have changed.

I put off going to the hotel. I wanted my night in Paris to be as short as possible. On the way down the Butte I saw, in a lighted *tabac*, a series of old postcards. I went in to buy some and discovered a traditional couscous restaurant, way off the tourist track. On impulse Geoff and I had a meal and talked about Modigliani. Did the postcards show the area as he'd seen it? He'd lived there between 1906 and 1909, and then in 1914 with Beatrice Hastings.

An old and very glamorous woman at the next table said, 'Excuse me, I heard you mentioning Modi. My mother was one of his models.'

So I explained that I was writing a book on the subject of his life and anything she could tell me would be most helpful. Her companion, a tough French businesswoman, was immediately hostile. As soon as I mentioned his name she turned against me: 'Writing a book about him. It's all been done.' It was like a slap in the face. Her hostility was quite sensational. I thought she must be one of the biographers' literary agents. She was in fact the agent of her companion, the old *vedette*, who still worked in cabaret.

So I asked which of the models had been her mother and she said the Italian girl, Elvira. She was the loveliest of his nude models, the most exotic. Some of the biographies suggested she was La Quique, a well-known Pigalle cabaret performer shot for espionage in the First World War. The *vedette* said that was someone else. 'Books? What do they know? My mother said he was the best lover she ever had.'

'What was he like? Did she tell you?'

'He was a poet, not of this life. He had such a childish radiance you forgave him anything.'

I asked greedily about Jeanne. The very name made her emotional: 'The sacrificed one. Sacrificed for his work. She chose to die with him. She let him absorb her personality, her spirit, her strength, so that he could be more peaceful, so that he had the fire to paint.'

'Did you know her?'

'Darling, how old do you think I am? Should I sue my plastic surgeon?' She indicated her pampered face. 'I know about Jeanne, that's all.'

'Did he love her?'

'He needed her purity – perhaps because he could defile it. Who knows? But she couldn't save him. How can you control a man like that? Lunia Chorosco said she did. She said she stopped him drinking. With her he got well.'

'Chorosco?'

'Lunia Czechowska married a Polish baron, Chorosco.'

'Did she love Modigliani?'

'Of course. But it pained Jeanne Hébuterne, so she went away. To get over him. Maybe he sent her away. Now she lives in the Midi, near Nice – unless she's dead.' She shuddered.

Her agent said, 'Of course she's dead. How many years do you think you've got left?'

To cheer herself up, the old *vedette* talked about Modigliani dying in his studio. 'Why were they alone? Because everyone abandoned them. He was impossible at the end. Drunk, bitter, morbid, violent. The nerves in his face were going, grimacing like this.' Mindful of her complexion, she performed a small example. 'Only she – Jeanne – was with him. She stayed. The Chilean painter found them – '

'Who told you?'

'André Salmon. And the *concierge*. It was known. But the dealer Zborowski had to make a good story in case Modigliani's family wanted to claim the pictures.'

Before she left she gave me the address of André Hébuterne, Jeanne's brother. She didn't know if he was still alive. She didn't know if she herself was still alive half the time, she said. Her agent folded her into a marvellous fur. The *vedette* business hadn't done her any harm. 'Perhaps you have to write about them, or you

13

wouldn't be doing it.' The agent friend looked displeased and wanted to go. The *vedette* added, 'You must remember, whatever you write, that he loved my mother. She was his true love. Look at the paintings.'

Then she left and Geoff said, 'And she's his daughter. She'll be saying that next.'

I could see that finding the truth even from the thoughts of those who actually knew him would be difficult because they all had an axe to grind, an ego to brighten, a claim to fame. In the ensuing months I heard of several women, one a countess who'd modelled for him – in later years she was a hunchback – she too had been his one true love.

Talking about him certainly caused a tension in other women. It was as though he was still around.

Morning came. Breakfast at the door. Then I received a bad call from Jacqueline. She was a dark bird of doom, antagonistic in every move and thought. We had a short quarrel. It was totally impossible for me to be at an appointment on the other side of Paris at 9 a.m., 8 my time. I couldn't even talk to myself at that hour. The appointment was to speak with the French art critic Jeanine Warnod. I told Jacqueline to make it later. She refused.

We arranged to meet a ninety-two-year-old man at his flat near Rond Point. His name was Raoul Leven and he'd been Cocteau's secretary. I asked Jacqueline if he did in fact know something about Modigliani. She'd taken me on so many false trails. It was as though she enjoyed it. She was always triumphant after disaster – someone else's. 'You must ask him before I set off,' I said.

'You ask him,' she snapped back.

I reminded her that I was paying her, so he'd better know something.

Geoff and I took photographs of the rue Lepic, where Modigliani would have walked constantly. We found doorways and side streets that would not have changed. It was a beautiful bright clear spring day, very cold. When I was fifteen I'd hung around Pigalle and the Montmartre area with my friend Beryl. How we'd envied the glamorous showgirls and models, and probably the whores. We were desperate to grow up and be movie stars. We'd worn black Bohemian arty clothes, modelled for painters, danced in the streets for money, slept in all-night cafés like The Black Cat, or on *métro* steps. When we did get money, instead of eating we bought a bottle of Worth toilet water, 'Je Reviens', which epitomised everything we wanted to be.

There was a definite smell of sadness in the air: a time that was gone. I didn't think it was my youth with Beryl. In Paris I felt I linked into some other state, one containing loss, pain, the unbearable. I couldn't define what it was. I did my best to ignore it. Normally I didn't let a place get me down. If it took me up, like New York, I was grateful. Places were just episodes I was passing through – normally.

Jacqueline was waiting near Raoul Leven's flat's entrance, looking like a man with long red hair and a bright blue suit. Her hair looked as if it had received a compliment forty years ago and had never forgotten it. That hair, obstinate like her, would never be cut. She greeted me by saying that if I thought some places were bad, this was thirty times worse. We crossed through a tiny passage like a lavatory and into a room that was in complete darkness. Too many of us were crowded together. There was just one dim light like the lamp of a small, lonely, distant boat at night. Raoul was standing supported by iron crutches that fitted on to his arms and as I went past, my bag strap caught over the circular top of one crutch. As I walked forward I nearly pulled him to his death. I had to retrieve my strap from his crutch, but in the dark I kept touching him in an intimate place. I couldn't see a thing. He was horrified.

'What are you doing, Madame? I'm ninety-two years of age.'

I explained that I'd got my bag caught on his crutch. Jacqueline said, 'Leave him alone. Why do you keep touching him like that? Are you sick?'

I supposed there was no light because he was suffering from some eye defect.

Geoff and I clung together like Babes in the Wood and got across to where the dim light shone. We found something flat, covered with newspapers. It looked like a bed. Jacqueline stood in a space, protecting her suit and hair. The man remained standing. It didn't look as though it would be a long interview. I began in French and explained the purpose of my visit. I got out my tape-recorder and asked if he minded. Then I said, 'What do you know about Modigliani?'

'I know nothing.' And without pausing he added, 'I knew everybody else, but not him.'

I could not see Jacqueline but felt her triumphant expression. It was a repetition of other old men she'd found. I'd travelled miles to sit in a dark room. I looked at her through the gloom and thought I'd kill her.

We stumbled into brilliant sunlight. She did look pleased with herself. Was she working for the French government? Did they think they owned the rights to Modigliani's life because he drank himself to death on their streets?

'It must be terrible being that old and blind,' I said.

'But he's not blind, *chérie*,' she crowed. 'He closed all his shutters because he didn't want you to see the dirt. My God. He lives in this *quartier*, like that.' She was certainly getting a sightseeing tour of squalor since beginning the Modigliani quest.

'You must have known he didn't have anything to say,' I said.

She laughed bitterly, like an angry bird. 'Perhaps he didn't want to tell you.'

I asked why she hadn't found out that he didn't know anything and so saved me a journey.

'It's for you to meet them and find out yourself.' She got a lot of amusement out of that. I let her go on laughing and decided not to pay her.

I stopped the cab and dropped her off near her flat. I agreed with Geoff that she was a load of trouble. He said, 'It's as though they're all trying to block you.'

I had to agree that the quest didn't have a generous feel about it.

We went to the rue Amyot, where Jeanne had lived with her parents and brother and where she'd died, aged twenty-one. As I turned off the rue Mouffetard into the rue Tournefort I almost recognised the place. It was like Gerona when I'd first gone there – the light, the smells, the atmosphere, the buildings. Even the sun came out and the sky was bright blue. It had the lovely innocence of something freshly discerned that could enrich my life. It wasn't at all like Paris. In fact, in the earlier streets the other side of Mouffetard the sky had been dull.

It was a trail back into the past – mine, Jeanne's. I stood opposite 8 rue Amyot. I looked at the doorway of 8 *bis*. Behind us was a courtyard with beautiful spring trees, flowers, a shed, a few seats and a building which looked like a school. I backed into the courtyard, where possibly Jeanne came to sit.

Then a *concierge* came out and gave a display of French manners, the sort that account for their bad name. What were we doing taking photographs? Get out.

I said it was for a book.

'I am desolate, Madame, but you can't take photographs without asking permission, so you'll have to go.'

Geoff took the last one defiantly, the door of 8 *bis* through the arch. A lovely lucky shot. Nothing much would have changed since the early 1900s. The only problem was – it didn't come out.

We took a taxi to meet Modigliani's niece Madame Schalit in the Michelangelo Molitor district. This was the Paris I knew, and the anguish flared up. I went rapidly into her flat. I wanted to get it over with and go back to London.

But Madame Schalit was full of good, clear, happy life. She had wonderful eyes – a real beauty at seventy-eight. I couldn't stop looking at her. I thought I could see her uncle in that smiling face. If he had her charisma I could see why they'd all been mad about him. Madame Schalit was blessed with life and life had been good to her, as no doubt it would have been to him if he'd not been tortured by art. He didn't deserve rejection and shabbiness; he deserved to look like her.

I asked Madame Schalit about Jeanne.

'She was very strong-willed and determined to be with him. She devasted her parents by her actions.'

'Was she strange? Mad?' Some accounts implied she was.

She laughed. 'No, it was him that was mad. All the Garsins are. It's their charm. People who are too direct are no fun.' Madame Schalit was a Garsin on her father's side. He was the brother of Eugenia, Modigliani's mother.

'Would he have married Jeanne?'

17

'Oh yes. They were going to marry in Cannes or Nice, but he died too quickly. He wrote to his mother that he would marry Jeanne.'

There was no published copy of that letter.

'Did the family object?'

She didn't know. She had never heard about it.

'Why did Jeanne kill herself?'

'She was too sad to live,' she answered deftly. The answers were so obvious – to her.

Later, Geoff and I went to the area where Modigliani had lived with Jeanne. We looked into the Rotonde, where he'd spent many hours sketching clients for a fixed sum of five francs. I looked at the photographs displayed inside – Kisling, Soutine, Foujita, Pascin – and I sought out his pictures.

I had difficulty finding the rue de la Grande Chaumière. Outside no. 8 was a plaque: 'Atelier Modigliani'.

We went to the end of the hallway and opened a glass-panelled door on to a courtyard with plentiful flowers, grass, a tree, a water tap. Children were playing on bikes. An old man wearing a beret watched us. 'Studio Modigliani?' He pointed to another, older building across the yard. I recognised the tree as the one in Jeanne Hébuterne's picture, the one various biographers had said she'd painted in Nice. Geoff pointed to the tap: 'She'd have got her water there.'

I knew from the books that he'd lived with Jeanne on the top floor. Ortiz de Zárate, the Chilean painter, was directly below in the studio once occupied by Gauguin. Modigliani and Jeanne had moved there in either July 1917 or July 1919, according to which book you read. Their daughter Jeanne said it was 1917. Lunia and Hanka Zborowski had decorated the studio and according to Lunia, in one account, Modi had cried with joy. His first home. In another of her accounts it was Jeanne who'd wept.

The second building had an atmosphere which I'd experienced when I went back to my primary school. It was in the air, a smell that enticed memories. In the case of my school I smelt the playtime break milk and plasticine. Here it reminded me of the places I'd gone to with José in Gerona province: old cafés, hotels, railway stations untouched since the last century. The fact that this building too was more or less untouched, with flaking green walls and white ceilings, pleased me. The stairs were very steep, curving upwards; the stairwell was dramatically high with a skylight at the top. On the first landing stood a wooden cupboard like a coffin. It looked as though it had always been there.

The building smelt of oil paint. As we were about to climb the last flight, a woman dressed to go out came down from Modigliani's landing. I asked her if we could see the studio. She said no one lived there. It was empty, had been for years. Nothing to see. She seemed determined to block us, yet she was quite polite. We asked if we could take photographs of the doorway. She wasn't keen and suggested if we went back into the first building we'd have a better view of his studio. I explained I was doing a book and wanted to see inside the studio briefly. She, alas, didn't have a key, she said. I must say I unearthed a lot of negative reaction in Paris.

We climbed to the door of what had been Modigliani's studio in the last months of his life. The window in the roof was still full of sun. Behind us, the steep coil of stairs and the patch of tessellated floor at the bottom – the very view Jeanne would have seen. There were two doors at right angles to each other and in front, the original doorway – only its frame was left. On the facing door was a poster for an exhibition. We looked through the keyhole. I could see orange light and floorboards. The place was empty. The door to the left had a shopping bag on wheels propped in front of it. I guessed that's where the woman had come from.

I went downstairs and knocked at Gauguin's former studio. A painter carrying a brush came to the door. Behind him was a room full of work. He was polite but busy and assured me the studio above was empty, had been for some years. There was nothing to see. So I described it as I felt it was inside: one room, then a small passage with something square or rectangular sticking out, then another further room. He said the sticking-out shape was a lavatory. Then I said, 'The room to one side with its own door. That was part of the original studio. It was at one time shaped like the letter L.' He seemed surprised I knew that. I wasn't surprised. I asked if he knew anything about Modigliani. He didn't. He was eager to get back to work. I had so many questions to ask, but of whom? I climbed the

19

stairs back to the top studio. Geoff was nervous. He said there was nothing in there.

I told him to get the door open. 'Use a credit card.'

He didn't like it but started on the lock of the facing door. Footsteps came towards the door on the left. From inside the room they came: fast, heavy steps, a determined walk, with a bounce. No lightweight, this person. We jumped back ready to run down the stairs. The steps stopped. The door did not open. Then the footsteps went away from the door to the interior of the room. Yet we'd been told no one was there. I tapped on the door, knocked – nothing. We hurried down the stairs, nervous now; my coat, with its luxurious fur collar and lining, dragging on the stairs like a slain animal. At the bottom I stopped and sat on the step. Through the glass-panelled door I could see the tree in the courtyard. I wanted to feel, to sense as much as I could. I wasn't really scared.

The sculptor Zadkine and Nina Hamnett had said they'd heard him after his death walking in the studio at night. They said he'd woken them. And other friends had said they felt he was there, on the street or in a café. It was as though he hadn't really gone, only from sight.

We crossed the courtyard into the first building at the moment the woman we'd seen earlier came through the front door carrying shopping. She was friendly this time and took us to see Georges Charaire, who would know the most about Modigliani. She pointed to a cat in the courtyard. 'Modigliani's cat,' she said. So she knew he'd had one. Georges wasn't in, so we stood on the stairs while I tried to persuade her to let us into her room – just to get a sense of the atmosphere. She suggested we should come the next day and she'd look out some cuttings and information about Modigliani. It said something for my complete absorption in what I was doing that I forgot I was in Paris, that I should get out, and agreed to call the following morning.

I asked what she knew about his life, and mostly what she said contradicted what I'd read. There seemed to be so many contradictions. I asked about their last week. She agreed that it was strange Jeanne hadn't gone for help. It was a compelling instinct to get help for someone. She shivered. 'I have heard that something terrible went on in there during those last days.'

20

I asked if she ever heard sounds of footsteps or doors being opened.

She laughed. 'No.' Then she moved quite abruptly up the stairs. She half-turned to look at me. 'You don't look English, Madame.'

'So what do I look?'

'I'd have said French. You don't look the same as you did earlier this afternoon.'

It was seven in the evening and we started back towards Pigalle to meet my friend Charlotte. On impulse I stopped the taxi at the address given to me by the *vedette* the night before. André Hébuterne, Jeanne's brother, lived in the rue de Seine. I had to see him.

Again I climbed stairs. They lived at the top of a high old building. An old woman spoke from behind the door, which remained shut. I said I needed to talk about Jeanne Hébuterne. She wouldn't let me in. She was ill, she said. Her voice was quite clear and contained. She said she knew nothing about Jeanne. Yes, I was talking to André Hébuterne's wife. He had nothing whatsoever to say. It all happened a long time ago. 'My husband was away at war. You probably don't remember it.'

I remembered it ended in 1918, not 1920.

I said there was an injustice and I wanted to put it right. She said there was nothing to say. It was a long time ago.

So I hung around on the stairs and Geoff still waited one flight below. I heard André Hébuterne's voice, soft, almost musical with extreme age. It was as though it came from another sphere. He was so old, did it matter any more? Yes, secrets of the past. They mattered. And I heard what I had to – enough to make me see it wasn't as written and would never be. The wife sounded angry: '*Le cas Hébuterne*. Will it never stop?'

I thought: not until it is stopped. I couldn't hear all she said.

On the way down the stairs Geoff and I met an old woman coming up. I was beginning to realise that I would meet everyone on the stairs in this story. I said I had been visiting the Hébuternes. She was happy about that and prepared to be friendly. She was the sister of André's wife. Her piercing bright eyes missed nothing.

On impulse I said I was writing a book about Jeanne. All

friendliness was suddenly gone, but she shook my hand, then Geoff's. 'Bravo. I wish you luck.'

'So you think the truth should be told?'

'If you ever find the truth.'

'It's a complicated story, Madame,' I said.

'You could say that.' And she gestured. 'Very.'

She opened the door to her flat, prepared to go in. I could see that the place was well ordered, even opulent. 'Do you ever think of Jeanne?' I was trying to keep her, hold her attention, stop her closing the door.

'No, I do not. That abominable, terrible suicide.' She was angry, upset. She started to close the door, then hesitated, staring at me as though I was some despairing spirit unable to find rest. Is that what they look like? She wanted to know. One last curious look, then she shut the door firmly.

I said, 'I expect Jeanne got a lot of this. Doors in her face. When she went off with him.'

Back in London I received copies of some of Jeanne Hébuterne's letters from Madame Prud'hon and a copy of the unpublished photograph of Jeanne. Reading the letters, I saw she was not at all as depicted in published accounts.

Then came the business of the bangle. I could see it clearly in my thoughts – quite wide, made of a thick pink glass and decorated with dark green leaves and mauve flowers. The leaves were outlined in a darker colour. The word 'lalique' accompanied this image. It was not a word I'd come across, and I supposed lalique was the name of the glass material. The bangle would not go away. Whatever I did it returned with insistence. It came at the time I read the letters. Finally I phoned Madame André Hébuterne and she actually spoke to me about Jeanne. I quoted what she herself had said on the phone to my assistant, Jacqueline. 'Many things have been said and written – some right. A lot wrong.' I added, 'I want to write the truth.'

She replied with the pat answers she'd used in so many interviews on the subject, so I gave her a question she wasn't prepared for. 'Madame, do you think he was good for Jeanne?'

'How could he be? He was a drunk.'

22

'So you think it would have been better if she hadn't gone with him?'

'Ask yourself that,' she replied brusquely.

'You could tell me.'

'Of course it would have been better if she'd left him.'

'It would have been better if she'd lived?'

'I wasn't there, Madame.' She sounded very definite.

'Was the family very shocked?'

'Very!'

'But the relationship had given them many shocks. Perhaps the outcome was not so surprising.'

'They wanted nothing to do with it, Madame.'

I described the pink bangle. She paused, then said, 'That was many years ago. Years ago.'

I wanted to ask who'd given it to Jeanne, but she was worried. How could I know about an object from so long ago? She was silent. Then she said, 'The child was brought up properly in Italy and given a good education. She was not neglected. So there is no problem.'

'But that's not true. She had an unhappy time with Margherita, his sister. Far too rigid. She died a drunk.'

'I am very sorry to hear that,' she said.

I made a million phone calls to Georges Charaire to make sure he'd be there and that it was agreed I could see the studio. My friend Stewart came with me and we arranged to take a train to Dieppe straight after the meeting with Georges.

When I reached the crossroads by the Dôme and the Rotonde, I just could not find the rue de la Grande Chaumière. It was as though it had disappeared. I kept crossing over the boulevards, the streets, but every angle looked the same. Stew, irritated beyond belief, kept saying, 'But you've been here before. Twice. Are you sure it exists?'

I felt nervous because I normally have a good sense of direction and don't get roads wrong. Suddenly I was disorientated. It took half an hour and the help of the Rotonde waiter to find the doorway, a mere three minutes away.

Georges, warm and generous, was pleased to see me. His friend Roger D, who owned the studio, told anecdotes about the old days in Montparnasse: 'Modi never paid his rent. Instead he offered my grandfather a canvas, saying, "In ten years it will be worth a hundred times the rent." How was my grandfather to know he was telling the truth? All the artists said they were geniuses. How was he to know which one was right? It was like backing a horse. After Modi's death my grandfather kicked himself. He had plenty of company. Rosalie, who ran the *crémerie*, had let rats chew thousands of dollars' worth. Every other meal she gave him was paid for with a painting. If my grandfather had taken just one in lieu of rent I wouldn't be here today, I tell you. I'd be in the South Seas.' He still insisted that Jeanne jumped from a studio window, and said he'd show me which one. She'd in fact fallen from the window in the rue Amyot.

Then they talked about Rosalie and how she loved Modi and kept throwing him out. 'She slept with him,' Roger told Georges in argot.

'Who didn't?' said Georges.

'What about Jeanne?' I asked.

'He treated her differently to the others,' said Georges. 'She was a madonna. Having his children. He respected that.' He then remembered Ortiz de Zárate saying she was always loyal, loyal to the end – and after the end. When Ortiz visited, he noticed that Modi treated her tenderly. 'During the war there was no money and no food, but there was heat made by the friends. We'd gather together. A community.'

I wondered how old that made him. As well as great warmth, did he also have the secret of eternal youth?

Finally we climbed the stairs to the locked empty studio. There was no sign of the woman in the adjoining room. It was unchanged since Jeanne's time.

'Why is the studio empty?' I asked Roger.

'It needs a lot of work.' And Georges indicated a broken floorboard.

Back downstairs, Georges got busy pouring drinks. Roger was stubborn about the suicide. He didn't like being denied the chance to promote a piece of the legend on his property. 'It happened here. My grandfather described it.'

I told him about the workman pushing the body around Paris on a handcart.

Georges said, 'You know more about it than anyone.'

'Possibly.'

'It's a Greek tragedy,' said Georges.

At the end of January 1989 I went with Stewart to south-east France. I wanted to go somewhere 'new', somewhere I'd never been before. I wanted new sensations, atmosphere, people – somewhere that would give nourishment and pleasure. My ex-husband, who lives in France, suggested Aix-en-Provence. The suggestion was approved of by people who'd been there. The more I heard about Aix, the more I wanted to visit. Because of the Monte Carlo Rally and a pop publication congress in Cannes, the planes to the area were all full. So we flew to Lyon, another new place, the gourmet capital of France. I decided to stay two nights, take the train to Aix-en-Provence, then go to Gerona briefly before flying back to London.

On the second morning in Lyon, having breakfast in my room, I noticed the low iron railing on the balcony outside the window. As I was looking at its engraving, quite casually, with the winter sun shining in, it all came back – the Jeanne business. And I thought: this is near the time that she went to the railing outside her window and down into the street below. My mind shifted to Modigliani and I could see, as though in front of me, a room full of smoke and people. He was there, eloquent and elegant, and I'm sure Lunia was there, and the dealer Zborowski.

We ate lunch in Brasserie Georges, which had such a reliable, trustful atmosphere; its food beyond reproach, it was a favourite with the townspeople. Then we went to catch the Marseille train. We could take one from the Gare Perrache, next to our hotel, but I could see from the timetable that it was better to cross town to the Gare Part-Dieu; from there a train left at 13.45 and arrived, without stopping, in Marseille forty minutes earlier than the Perrache train. I asked the girl at Reception which was the best train. I also asked the cab driver. I was doing a lot of checking up.

I bought the tickets and checked with the salesgirl that the train for Marseille left from platform G. When we got on to the platform, Stewart noticed that Marseille wasn't on the board.

'But the first stop is Marseille. It's in the book: 13.45.' There was no other train leaving at that time. The board showed only Toulon,

Cannes and Nice. Obviously they didn't put up every station. There was no problem.

We got on the train, which turned out to be a TGV – the crack train, the fastest – and didn't have seats available in first class. There were two skimpy seats in second class, or we could sit in first opposite the lavatory.

I explained to the ticket collector that I'd booked first-class seats. He was a weasel-faced, sly-looking individual, like a bad character from Proust. He followed me as I trailed up and down the train, saying only one thing in ever-increasingly aggressive tones: 'Supplément!'

I refused the seats near the lavatory. I wanted to see the view outside the window. After all, it was a new view. I handed him a 100 franc note, which at last shut him up. 'Two for Marseille.'

'But this train doesn't stop at Marseille.'

I wouldn't believe it. I needed someone to blame, and looked at Stewart. He wasn't keen on blame, and anyway he wanted to get to Aix-en-Provence, not Toulon, which was the train's first stop.

The ticket collector made plans: 'You will have to get off at Toulon and wait for the Marseille train. To get to Aix-en-Provence you then take a bus, but by the time you get to Toulon and back I don't know if the bus will still be running. It is Sunday.' He described an impossibly long journey only he could think up. I couldn't bear to hear any more of his bad news and dragged to and fro, first and second, looking for seats. Why couldn't they get the timetable sorted out? Why didn't the ticket salesgirl concentrate on what I was asking and she was saying? I dragged my coat with its famous fur collar in one hand and it trailed behind me, sometimes on the floor, at others catching on seats. Buttons fell off. And then, in my fury, I sat on it and a lapel tore. On that journey it fell to pieces. It simply died. I said bitterly, 'I'm not meant to have luxuries. That's obvious.'

And then I saw it: Nice. Of course it was no coincidence. I was going to Nice after all. All the memories returning, the wrong train. I'd never taken a wrong train in my life, even drunk. I thought: I'm supposed to go there, and that's it. And it made sense to go on rather than stop at Toulon, an unattractive place. We should go to Cannes and stay the night. But I remembered the Monte Carlo Rally and the pop publication congress and realised the hotels would be full.

So we stopped at Cagnes-sur-Mer, a small seaside place just before Nice. The ticket collector said we could get a hotel there. So I paid another supplement and he looked like a happy weasel. To cheer me up he said, 'You will be having dinner in Cagnes-sur-Mer instead of trying to find a coach for Aix.'

I did ask myself: should I go on or should I go back? How I'd tried to get to Nice in November 1987, before beginning the book! How many attempts had been blocked! Yet here I was, taken almost against my will. I had to accept the idea that sometimes life does take over.

In the biographies the emphasis was on Nice. That's where they stayed and Jeanne's baby was born. Nice was where she'd lived with her mother, while he stayed in a prostitutes' hotel. Nice was what I'd remembered. Not Cagnes. I did recall Modigliani staying in Cagnes with the Osterlinds – Anders Osterlind was a painter and his wife Rachèle was dying of intestinal tuberculosis. And the group of artists that Zborowski had brought to the Midi . . . Foujita and his wife . . . Soutine had swum in the Mediterranean. He was very excited because it was the first time he'd seen the sea. And Osterlind had taken Modigliani to visit Renoir, and the visit had been unsatisfactory.

When we got off the train it was dark. Stew told the cab driver to take us to a hotel near the sea. We were getting into the cab when I said, 'What about up? Is there an up? Hills? Mountains?'

The driver said St-Paul-de-Vence. That didn't sound right. 'It's very chic. Film stars live there.'

I still wanted to go up. I felt there was a place that looked over a bay.

'You mean Haut-de-Cagnes.'

That was the name I wanted to hear.

As I arrived in Haut-de-Cagnes under cover of darkness, I believed what I saw: an untouched fortress village, dominated by a château overlooking the Baie des Anges. As the taxi scraped through narrow cobbled streets to the only hotel open, I tried to remember where in Cagnes the Osterlinds had lived. Was it by the sea or up here? The hotel was so expensive that even the cab driver, used to ferrying millionaires to and from their villas and Nice airport, gestured extravagantly. I thought this visit should be a short one.

27

The hotel was a de luxe but complicated establishment with a lot of history on show. It had an Alice in Wonderland feel to it – that was the most complimentary way of describing it. The place had more than a suggestion of a clip joint. The girl at Reception had a cheerful, rough manner that didn't go with the prices. I said I wanted information about the Osterlinds, who'd lived in Cagnes during the First World War. She reached for a phone book and asked how to spell Osterlind. I explained that as they'd been mature adults in 1919 it was unlikely they were still alive. Obviously an optimist, she still looked in the phone book. I said the mayor's office would have records and asked for that number. I told her I was doing a book on Modigliani and wondered if anyone in the village had information. The girl said, 'He stayed here.'

'Modigliani? Here?' I was amazed.

'In the blue room.' Playfully she handed me a key. 'You've got it.'

Never a slouch for a coincidence, I didn't, however, go for this one. What was a destitute painter doing in a hotel? I asked the date of his stay. Obviously she wasn't around to remember personally. No longer sure of herself, she switched celebrities.

'Simone de Beauvoir also stayed in the blue room.'

'But she's dead.'

'Of course, Madame.' And she gave me a hotel brochure on which Modigliani's name featured prominently with Renoir, Soutine and Foujita.

The blue room certainly looked old. The only problem – that part had been built in 1987. The air was marvellous and I felt optimistic, euphoric. The village was deserted – three cats at most. By day it was a discouraging place because it had been bought up by wealthy foreigners who spent at most a few weeks a year in residence. The emptiness of the night before was not caused by people retiring early – the indigenous inhabitants couldn't afford to live there. Darkness made the village magical. In the light of day it had the shrieking falseness of a stage set: one shop open selling postcards and souvenirs and many tourist restaurants, all empty. Further down the steep hill leading to Cagnes-sur-Mer there was a closed grocery store with crates of vegetables in various states of well-being stacked outside. The houses were over-restored. It was all pretty enough, but unreal. Tourism was the main stock in trade, and art ran a close second.

Well-heeled artists blended with their rich patrons. Art was run by the *conservateur*. He was responsible for the regular Château exhibitions and knowing who was in this artists' paradise of the migrating rich. It was to him I turned for the Osterlinds' address.

He was sitting in his office, chock-full of uncouth pride. Two assistants, both women, looked as though they took a lot of orders.

'Osterlind!' He waved a hand dismissively. I mentioned Modigliani. It was as though I'd spat in his face. 'We have no time for Modigliani here.'

His answer surprised me considerably. 'But I'm talking about Modigliani the Italian painter.' Was there perhaps some disgraced ex-inhabitant of the same name?

'Who needs him here? We have Renoir.'

'He stayed with the Osterlinds in 1919 – '

'He was never in this area. There is no proof. I am an artist, Madame, and I have my own work to do.'

Perplexed, I went to the house of a local art critic and painter. He was dressed in the style of a Haut-de-Cagnes painter, expensive and acceptable. But they always spoil it. Around his neck hung something large and silly on a chain. Around the room his paintings were stacked, desiring attention. On occasions like these I am very grateful that I'm short-sighted.

'Modigliani!' It was as though I was asking for Satan. 'He was never here. He was in Nice. You've got it wrong.' And he picked out a book of Modigliani's work and turned to a landscape, one of the two he'd painted. 'This was supposed to have been painted here. I've searched the area and failed to find it.' He slammed the book shut.

The next morning I went to see Ulla Fribrock, a Swedish painter who had been married to the son of Emile Lejeune, a Swiss painter. She said he had known Modigliani, in Cagnes and Montparnasse. Ulla pointed across to the house renovated by the mayor's daughter. Before the 'restoration' she had done several paintings of what was then a mysterious white house, flanked by trees. 'It had a certain magic when I went inside, so I was not surprised he'd lived there. His daughter was born in that house in 1919.'

It had always been understood that the baby was born in Nice hospital. I found it a change that one inhabitant wanted to claim not only Modigliani but members of his family too.

'He was not the degenerate drunk they make him out to be here. He was a *grand seigneur.*' For a while Modigliani had lived in a Nice hotel frequented by prostitutes. They had posed for him and looked after him when he was ill. Emile had taken that story no further.

Ulla gave me a book on Soutine by Lanthenam which contained a chapter on Modigliani saying he was an initiate of cabala. Having been involved with José's return of Sephardic mysticism to Gerona, I'd learnt from rabbis and scholars that cabala was not a quick business and required years of learning and experience. When, I wondered, had the painter fitted this in? Lanthenam backed up his assertion by drawing attention to the mystical signs Modigliani sometimes marked on the sides of paintings. I thought that came from reading Nostradamus, which he did avidly, as was the custom in France at that time. He was also familiar with tarot and had an exchange on the subject with the poet and writer Max Jacob, who practised astrology. In the studio, a chart for the baby Jeanne was found amongst his possessions. Ulla asked me to keep the book, which I thought very kind as it was out of print and rare. Lejeune had said that Modigliani didn't always sign his name because he found it too long.

I'd been led to Haut-de-Cagnes, but for what? I had no desire to go to Nice. I thought it might contain bitter memories and could turn into Paris-on-sea.

Back in London, I quickly established from research material that Modigliani had resided at several addresses in Cagnes. Jeanne, her mother and the group of artists had lived in two villas owned by Curel. One, called 'Le Pavillon des Trois Sœurs', was certainly in Haut-de-Cagnes: 'It was set high on a hill behind the village of Cagnes with a good view of the Mediterranean.' Because Modigliani missed Paris he spent time looking for a suitable bar and found one high up by the château in Haut-de-Cagnes, owned by Mademoiselle Rose. It had no windows and resembled a cave. He liked its disorderly atmosphere and Rose, considered a harpy, allowed him credit. But she was contemptuous of the drawings he gave in exchange.

There was no mystery about where Osterlind lived: the house was just above Renoir's. Modigliani had arrived one day, 'with the beautiful features of an Italian prince but was tired and dirty . . . With him, his shadow, the poetic Zborowski, who in brotherly friendship wanted to keep him from the dangerous life of Nice.' And Osterlind went on to say that he gave him his best room, in which he produced some beautiful work. It was near Osterlind's house that Modigliani saw the Pernod advertisement which so impressed him: '*Mon vieux!* They never made anything more beautiful than that.'

Then Madame Prud'hon in Paris found previously unseen drawings by Jeanne Hébuterne. They were there amongst her mother's effects. She found them while I was in Cagnes, and thought I should have them.

I was excited, but also uneasy. Madame Prud'hon was very keen to reproduce Jeanne's work, and eager that I should write this account. She said, 'The picture of Jeanne is not correct. She was not the odd victim they made her out to be. She had such precision.' She had changed her earlier statement about Jeanne. 'I said odd because that's what my aunt had told me. But then my aunt came from a different background and to her, artists would appear strange.'

I asked about the pink bangle that I had seen so clearly. Had her mother Germaine Labaye ever mentioned it?

'My mother hardly spoke about Jeanne. She was too upset – even years later, when the daughter Jeanne Modigliani came to see her. She never got over her friend's death.'

And so I had discovered letters written by Jeanne to her best friend, Germaine Labaye. I had talked to the daughter's widow about what she had later discovered, and to the remaining children, whose parents had known Jeanne; and finally to her brother André's wife. I had in front of me a different picture. And then other material had come to light – her line drawings, photographs, part of her diary, her mother's notes, unknown rivals. The silence was broken. It was time to place Jeanne in her true light. What I learned and what people told me I then put into the following story. The evidence is in the tale.

And I wish to thank those who haven't spoken before, who have trusted me.

Exposition

Chapter One

'It would have been better for everyone if she'd never met him. She gave us all a look into hell. That terrible, terrible suicide.' This was how a relative of Modigliani's last mistress summed up one of the most turbulent tragedies of the art world. Jeanne Hébuterne's suicide stayed indelibly in the minds of those who'd known her. Seventy years later those few who remained, or their children, behaved as though it had happened yesterday. In this case time could not heal.

When she died she was at the beginning of her life, only twenty-one, a promising artist, intelligent, sensitive, valued. She had a small daughter by Modigliani and was about to give birth to their second child. Modigliani had died the evening before, on 24 January 1920, in the Charity hospital Montparnasse, in great pain, penniless, drunk, a failure, his art unrecognised. Early the following morning Jeanne, nine months pregnant, went to the fifth-floor window of her parents' flat and fell to her death. She died because she could not live without him.

For the past week they'd been shut away, abandoned in an icy studio with only tins of sardines to eat, alcohol to drink. He was dying. Tubercular meningitis had set in. No one came near them. The mystery surrounding their deaths has never been resolved.

Jeanne was born on 6 April 1898 to Catholic parents in Arras, northern France. They later moved to the Mouffetard area of Paris and her father, Achille Casimir Hébuterne, worked as chief cashier in the perfumery department of the Bon Marché store. His origins were in North Africa; he was a Catholic convert, hardworking, pious, and he liked to be seen doing the respectable thing. Modigliani's brother met him after the tragedy in 1920 and said he was 'an inoffensive little man in a frock coat with a goatee beard. The typical Frenchman of 1900 with ideas to match.' Jeanne's mother, Eudoxie Anaïs, was considered 'solid'. Jeanne's brother André, born in 1894

35

in Meaux, Seine-et-Marne, choosing art as a profession, created the first crack in their invincible respectability. The father, an ardent admirer of Pascal, read extracts as the family peeled potatoes for dinner and this, according to Germaine Labaye, irritated Jeanne. Her mother preferred Plotinus, a mystic writing of man's unification with God. When Jeanne followed her brother into the colourful milieu of Montparnasse, Monsieur Hébuterne realised that constant church-going and the reading of moral tracts would not keep his daughter in – or sin out.

Although the Hébuterne household has been labelled repressive, tyrannical, it is clear from Jeanne's teenage letters to Germaine that her mother was her good friend and on occasion kept a welcoming house. Jeanne writes in a light-hearted way of the Chambet couple whom Germaine will meet if she accepts Madame Hébuterne's invitation for dinner at six o'clock on Sunday 22 October 1916.

As a child Jeanne showed an aptitude for drawing and design, and in her early teens she studied at the Académie Colarossi in the rue de la Grande Chaumière, where she was later to live with Modigliani, and the École des Arts Décoratifs. She loved music and played the violin – her neighbourhood, the Mouffetard, was the violin-making area of Paris. She liked clothes and creating unique arrangements of colour and fabric. They were exotic, with oriental influence. She sought her own style rather than going for the fashionable thing. She enjoyed modern music, walking, going out with her friends, gossip, parties. At the same time she was reflective, and very perceptive and honest in her assessments of herself. She wanted her art to flourish and be exhibited. In 1915 she tried Chéron, one of the most important dealers in Paris. At that time he was Modigliani's dealer, though with little success.

Jeanne suffered lapses of concentration and sometimes felt so discouraged that she couldn't bear to look at her work, so she'd switch from life drawing to 'cartons', or go off to the countryside. She was in turn contemplative, practical, wry, extrovert. She could change her state of mind rapidly from thoughts of the material, to the mystical, to the sensual. She was certainly interested in men and the effect she had on them. She was profoundly influenced by the atmosphere of a place or district: it had a tangible effect on her, not always agreeable. She literally absorbed atmosphere – the absolute

36

unmarked whiteness of the walls surrounding her became fused with her, until she became a part of the whiteness, as though 'I have no reason to be'. Her fusion with Modigliani was like that. It was an almost mystical experience. Cidery fumes filling the room overwhelmed her. The shape of the girls' legs in Brittany moved her deeply, as did the colour of the autumnal trees, the same red as Germaine's chignon. She wasn't afraid to show affection and warmth and to be open with either sex.

The grey steely sea, the wet shoe-killing mud of Brittany, the smoke and sensation of the Rotonde café – they formed the sensual background to the piercing thoughts of disquiet and longing and the practical concerns about cost or the reflective ones about her brother in the war. Weather and temperature affected her strongly. She loved going out in whipping winds, getting soaking wet. She disliked the heaviness of certain air. It didn't suit her. Things that didn't suit her she described as 'suffocating'. In Paris she'd suddenly become stifled and long for the country grass. At the coast, which she found 'eternally beautiful', she'd suddenly yearn for the atmospheres of Montparnasse. She wrote that she chose to go out in violent weather. She wanted to go to extremes. There was a certain wildness in her.

She was highly sensitive to smells, finding them evocative and sometimes contradictory. As she lay in bed in a cheap hotel where she'd had the stained mattress removed – Modigliani had just left the room – she read a prose poem and conjured up the smell of the roses described. But then she was 'assailed by the voluptuous odour of urine' in the unemptied chamberpot in the bedside table – the door of which would not close. She lived a life of the senses which she described, drew, painted, and occasionally sculpted. She collected postcards of the small villages in Brittany which she called 'my harvest of images', and couldn't wait to show them to Germaine.

In the summer of 1914 no one believed the war could last. It would be over in two months. But then the Germans looked as though they were winning and the French army retreated. Paris seemed threatened, about to be evacuated. The main streets and boulevards were emptied of traffic. There were no newspapers; crowds gathered at the kiosks and read single-page handouts with the latest news. Tourists were gone. The big hotels were empty.

On 29 August Paris was bombed from the air for the first time. The city was now under blackout, and air-raid wardens and police were on the streets. Planes bombed Paris every day.

The war changed Montparnasse. The majority of the artists went to fight. Before they left, a party was given. The parties got wilder. Everyone stayed drunk. The foreign artists were left behind: Picasso, Gris, Archipenko, Foujita, Soutine, Kremagne, Kikoine, Lipchitz and the mad, debonair Ortiz de Zárate. Neither Max Jacob nor Utrillo, both French, went. Ossip Zadkine enlisted later on and Kisling, who didn't have to, joined the Foreign Legion. Apollinaire went into the artillery. He and Braque were seriously wounded. Dr Paul Alexandre went into the medical service.

During the war years, before she met Modigliani, Jeanne's life had been divided between Paris and the country, where the local people posed for her. Her girlfriends were mostly art students. Germaine, Chana Orloff, Thérèse, Levy saw each other regularly and had the same interests. They talked about clothes, especially Poiret, the master of fashion. Jeanne was fascinated by oriental styles and made too many purchases in the Galeries Lafayette. They discussed art, the latest music, the stars of the Rotonde, the Dôme, and Closerie des Lilas, the influence of the Russian ballet and Bakst, the successful women painters Suzanne Valadon and Marie Laurencin, mistress of Guillaume Apollinaire. The letters they wrote to each other were delivered the same day. There were few telephones. They went to the artists' balls, they had 'amazing entertainments' in their homes with 'ultramodern music', and they used the term 'chic'.

Some of Jeanne's male friends she met through her brother. The Italian Futurist painter Severini knew her well and was interested in her work. The Japanese painter Foujita saw her in the cafés. A conspicuous figure in Montparnasse, small, with black fringed hair and hornrimmed glasses, he wore gold earrings and a dab of moustache under his nose. He studied the Greek way of life in Raymond Duncan's school. At times he wore a kimono, at others he affected a toga and garlands and went to dance classes under the trees. Stanislav Fumet had known Jeanne since childhood. There is mention of Chambet, Briot, and in one letter to Germaine, sent from the Rotonde, Jeanne is 'accompanied by Raphael'. The sculptor Leon Indenbaum was her friend. He also, independently, knew Modigliani. Jeanne was not a luminary of café life but a minor figure, noticeable nevertheless in her exotic turbans, brown cape and long boots. Indenbaum described her at that time as a 'dedicated young woman of character and substance. She had a beautiful soul. She was pretty in her fine way, not at all shy but secretive, proud, upright. She was fine, ethereal, delicate but not sick-looking. A small woman who did not give the impression of being small.'

Briot said: 'She has the eyes of a seeker. She will go far.'

Jeanne had a pale oval face, long plaits and slightly slanted blue-green eyes. No one could agree on their exact colour, or the precise shade of her hair. Indenbaum, who was the most reliable, said it was fair. It certainly had red reflections and could sometimes look brown. But those who remember her, including Germaine, Emile Lejeune and Marevna Vorobev, describe her as fair. She was nicknamed 'Noix de Coco' – Coconut – because of her hair colour. Germaine, a redhead, was called 'Haricot Rouge' – Red Bean.

Her skin could be so pale, almost waxen, that it ceased to resemble flesh. She held her small body well, with grace. She was compared to certain statues of madonnas in Chartres. She was described constantly as mysterious, possessing an almost mesmerising gaze.

Descriptions of Jeanne vary. She did provoke a contradictory response, both in appearance and manner – and this from people who must have seen her the same week. Either she experienced strange physical changes or she was a chameleon. Germaine's sister, still alive, said, 'Jeanne Hébuterne was strange. In her ways, her manner of speaking. Many people found her strange.' But Germaine's sister was not part of the art world, and as Germaine's daughter pointed out, artists were very different then. They were Bohemian and exclusive and lived by their laws. They did not blend into society as they do today.

The impression Jeanne made on those who didn't know her well is strangely at odds with the person who wrote to Germaine and liked parties. Modigliani's biographers depict her as humble, modest, clinging, a victim. This was what irritated her daughter, Jeanne Nechtschein, so much that she was compelled to write her book about her parents, stripping them of myth and legend – or trying to. She encountered a wall of silence. She said that in spite of what had been written about her mother, she had a strong, definite personality and a straightforward way of looking at people. Indenbaum added that she was not afraid to stand up for herself and meet their eye. The timidity and appalling lethargy referred to by some Modigliani biographers are not corroborated by her friends or family. Under threat, she became quiet. She was also a good listener. She was fascinated by most of what Modigliani had to say. Some of her acquaintances, like the painter Gabriel Fournier, who lived nearby, say they never remembered her speaking.

What is surprising is that Hanka Zborowski, who saw Jeanne repeatedly over a period of months in the South of France, could not remember hearing her say one word. Yet from Jeanne's friends' accounts she was talkative, even witty. Had sleeping with Modigliani struck her dumb? She was certainly able to leave his bed and do a financial deal for Germaine in the Rotonde in July 1917 which involved plenty of words and a certain amount of slang in the bargaining. And her letters show that she was open and unreserved. The most likely conclusion is that Jeanne Hébuterne could appear aloof to some, yet warm and life-loving to others.

Jeanne's letters to Germaine, whom she called 'Bibi', became more intimate and confiding over the years. At sixteen she sent a polite note asking Germaine to come and pose for her. She stated the time and what Germaine should wear. Her attitude to Germaine became affectionate but sensible: she took her in hand. Germaine, it appeared, had no sense of time or money or, sometimes, location. She even forgot to give her address in the country so that Jeanne could reply to her letter. They planned excursions which mostly came to nothing. One did look promising, and Jeanne wanted to know exactly what it would cost to get there, to stay, and how interesting the landscape was. Germaine, not bothered with practicalities, replied vaguely. Jeanne wanted concrete facts that her friend could not provide. She was in the habit of weighing up the worth of an action. There was no reason for her to change when she lived with Modigliani. He was worth the torment.

Jeanne also had a close relationship with her brother. Her friend Chana Orloff recalled how Jeanne and André would pay her visits, how adoring he was of his sister – in those days! 'Later,' said Chana, 'he condemned her without pity.'

When she wasn't in the country, Jeanne frequented the Bohemian hang-outs – the cafés, Marie Wassilieff's canteen, Rosalie's – but her life, that of a bourgeois French girl, was very different from that of the artists, especially the numerous foreigners who got by without heat in tormentingly cold winters and queued to wash at the Rotonde lavatory sink. They'd sit in the café all day to keep warm over one café crème and a shared sandwich. They relied on servicemen and tourists coming to look at 'the artists', to buy their drawings. The café proprietor didn't object to the small order because the artists were an attraction. Many of the group were away: Kisling, Léger, Apollinaire were at the war. Modigliani, his health too bad for enlistment, was certainly in Paris. He was broke, because the war meant that his monthly postal order from his mother could not be sent.

The war brought curfews, rationing. Writing in *New Age* in 1914, Beatrice Hastings said the cafés closed at 8 p.m. and only the men walked about at night. Then absinthe was forbidden.

After the cafés closed the artists went to each other's studios, taking a few bottles. Everyone went to Rosalie's or Marie Wassilieff's to eat. By 1917, Foujita said the canteen had a certain snob interest. It had a cosmopolitan impromptu air – a distillation of Bohemia.

41

Jeanne's life, however, was regular. She walked in the Tuileries every evening, every Sunday afternoon, almost a constitutional. She made clothes, shopped and ate three meals a day. Her family were not wealthy, but they had enough. Her father was mostly posted out of Paris, and often they didn't know where until the last moment. Jeanne joined with the family in prayers for those at war, especially her brother. She was always waiting for news of him. When would he come home on leave? Would it be cancelled at the last minute? How long would he have? Planning her life was dependent on his visits. He was also friendly with Germaine and she was the only one loyal to him after Jeanne's suicide.

The Hébuternes were not as sophisticated as some of Jeanne's friends' families. André Hébuterne stated in 1989 that both Jeanne's and his background was normal. His wife Georgette reiterated 'normal' – ten times! She said, 'They were well brought up, properly educated, like anyone else. I see nothing abnormal about that.' Monsieur Hébuterne believed it was a normal household too. He went to work, earned his money, supported his family, did the right thing, served his country and belonged to the Church. Therefore his children should behave as he expected. It was a natural equation – for him. He could not believe that a child living under his influence, particularly a girl, could possibly behave as Jeanne did. It was the shock of his life, something only the Devil could be responsible for. But in those days, when she was fifteen, then sixteen, there was no reason to doubt that she would marry conventionally and live as her mother had. This art business was a mere girlish whim.

The period of blackout in Paris did not deprive the *quartier* of entertainment, and Jeanne mentions parties by invitation, dances and events to keep spirits up. There was a communal feeling in Montparnasse and the artists stuck together. Those French who were not artists, however, were growing restless. Many had lost sons and husbands at the Front, and disapproved of these foreign painters sheltering in their capital, taking the meagre amounts of food and coal they needed.

Jeanne was certainly a regular in the Rotonde and the other cafés long before she has been placed there by biographers. Sichel, the most accurate, assumes that she showed up in the spring of 1917. But in a letter dated 1915 she describes how the Rotonde terrace was boring, full of strangers, old men and models. All the interesting regulars were gone: 'Paris has become remarkably uninteresting.' At that time Modigliani was living with Beatrice Hastings, who had a house in the rue Norvins, Montmartre, and a flat in Montparnasse. Beatrice, an intellectual and man-eater, had independent means. Foujita said she loved eccentricity and carried a live duck around in a wicker basket. Blaise Cendrars, who had known Modigliani in his early years in Paris, said she was an 'hysteric . . . accosting all males and intoxicated from 9 p.m. on. She was infatuated with Modi.' Marie Wassilieff said, 'She was at first very beautiful with curly hair. Later she was more haggard than Modi.'

It has always been assumed that Modigliani was Jeanne's first and only love. Her first reference to a man she liked was in July 1915, when she was seventeen. She'd met him some time before in Marie Wassilieff's canteen and had already mentioned him to Germaine. 'He's a "type" my brother knows. I saw him again at Wassilieff's. I have made more ample acquaintance with him and with his friend, who's a musician. I see them a lot at the Rotonde.'

Modigliani was rarely absent from either place. It's not clear whether this 'type' was Modigliani, but he would certainly have seen Jeanne in the Rotonde or Marie Wassilieff's. And she would have seen him. It didn't need retrospect or tragic death to establish him as a café luminary. His entrances and exits were quite fabulous, at least in the earlier days when he left on his feet. In the later months his exits were not always vertical. He could be so flamboyant that his entrances resembled a commedia dell'arte performance, and he'd recite long passages of Dante, Baudelaire or Lautréamont in the streets at night. After his visit home to Livorno in 1913, he did not leave Paris for five years. Roger Wild, Germaine's husband, said he treated women with respect, and Jeanne was thirteen years his junior, untouched by sex or life. He did not rush her, even if she wanted him to. Their courtship, although irregular, lasted a conventional time. Roger said they knew each other as early as 1913.

Jeanne went to the Académie Colarossi: crowded, every room packed. The students were of all nationalities. The room where they drew from the nude was stuffy, overheated, the stove smoked, there was smoke from pipes and cigarettes, the model was sweating. It smelt of scent, fresh paint, sweating feet.

While Jeanne was studying there, Modigliani often showed up to sketch from the nude. If the 'type' was the Italian, then his friend the musician could have been Mario Varvogli, his last sitter before death. But that is speculation.

Jeanne had an emotional relationship with her art works which she shared with Germaine. She treated them personally. They irritated her, she wished she could lose them, forget they ever existed. She felt pleased with the way her spooning in clay gave her Aphrodite a 'superb stomach and stylish buttocks'. About Germaine's work she wrote:

> I understand that you are angry with your young girl. It would be without doubt preferable if she didn't exist. What do you think of this madonna which I send you? Don't you find she resembles a fruit? Contrary to you I am going to the countryside to escape from painting.

She described her works as though they had a separate life, as though they were naughty pets. She went to fetch the 'daubs' Chéron didn't want as though they were disgraced children.

Her line drawings undeniably showed talent. Severini said she was a fine artist. Foujita, Indenbaum, André Salmon the writer, Chana Orloff the sculptress – all saw that she was gifted. They saw it almost with surprise.

In retrospect, her friends said, 'She was waiting – all her life waiting for the big mystical experience that she was somehow born for. She was set on a path for exploration and creative work. She looked forward to life, expected to be happy.'

Then she fell in love with Amedeo Modigliani.

Chapter Two

Amedeo Modigliani – 'Modi' to his friends, 'Dedo' to his family and those who loved him – was born in Livorno, Italy, on 12 July 1884. He was the youngest of four children and his mother's favourite. His family, Italian Sephardic Jews, were well educated, especially on the mother's side, the Garsins, and from his maternal grandfather Modigliani received knowledge of the arts and sciences, well beyond what was available on the school curriculum. He discussed philosophy, ideas, history at an early age. His grandfather encouraged him to think – to widen perspective – to challenge the orthodox and reawaken the ancient and forgotten. The family were not afraid to be advanced and artistically lively. They didn't kowtow to the strictures of the bourgeoisie. They were sophisticated in their ideas, lively in discussion. Emanuele, the elder brother, later a Socialist Deputy, was vehemently political and went to prison for several months. Modigliani's love of poetry, interest in philosophy, fluency in expression, quick tongue, informed mind, were nurtured by those early influences.

His father failed at business and his mother took over the role of provider for the family by opening a school. In those days it was a brave thing to do. Modigliani didn't have much time for the traditional lessons at the local school – he'd already surpassed them years ago with his grandfather. He wanted to study art. He got his way. He had two serious illnesses in his teens – typhoid fever, then acute pleurisy, after which tuberculosis set in. His mother took him to the South of Italy on a long recuperative tour of the art centres of the world. He found a great affinity with the fourteenth-century masters and studied their technique, researched their ideas. At the same time he was taking an interest in women – it was reciprocal. He wrote letters to his guide and friend Oscar Ghiglia, eight years his senior, who (according to Margherita, Modigliani's sister) had started him along a path of drugs, mysticism, drink, spiritualism and sex. He then studied at Florence and Venice and began sculpting, which was

45

his first love. Throughout his life he was fascinated by Greek culture; he made many caryatids and planned to create a Greek temple. His influences were Greek and the Italian masters: Neroccio, Matteo di Giovanni, Simone Martini. Other influences were Egyptian statues and Assyrian and Chaldean art in the Louvre.

His mother persuaded his uncle in Marseille to fund his trip to Paris, every artist's dream, in 1906. Modigliani assured her he would make a name for himself. Here his vision would be realised.

He set himself up in some style in a hotel near the Madeleine, but his money ran out and with his elegant habits he was obliged to move to the Maquis, the poor artists' and vagrants' colony behind the Butte at the top of Montmartre. He started taking life-drawing classes at the Académie Colarossi and three of his paintings were exhibited in the Laura Wyldas art gallery. He thought he was on his way.

The following year he exhibited five watercolours and two oils in the Salon d'Automne, but Paris was not to be won. Its rejections were punishing. He turned more into himself, took to drugs and drink. There was no money except the allowance his mother managed to send and she supported him throughout his life, except during the war years when the money could not get through.

He moved from shack to hotel to park bench. For a while he worked in the artists' colony run by Dr Alexandre at the rue du Delta. His models – serving girls, seamstresses, prostitutes and the girls from the Montmartre bars – became his mistresses for one night. La Quique, a fiery, beautiful girl from Marseille, lasted longer. She and Modigliani were seen dancing naked by his shack in the Maquis. She was a flamboyant beauty, but she could not mitigate his growing sense of doom.

His one and only patron was Dr Alexandre, who bought some of the pictures and arranged commissions. Then Modigliani, in a rage, destroyed the artists' work at the Delta commune, after which he was disliked and excluded. He exhibited in the Salon des Indépendants, without critical notice or sale, and tried to find a dealer. He failed. His friends were Max Jacob and the painter Utrillo. Jacob had shared a room with, and supported Picasso. He was a fine poet, painted watercolours, had a brilliant mind. Modigliani respected him. He was an ether addict, a homosexual, a religious fanatic and a fortune-teller. Montmartre suited him and on his wall he'd scribbled 'Never go to Montparnasse'. He gave soirees in his impoverished room, wearing a frock coat, high hat and monocle. Maurice Utrillo was a lifelong friend of Modigliani. The illegitimate son of Suzanne Valadon, he was poor, alcoholic and became so ill he had to be shut away occasionally in a mental hospital. Picasso and his acolytes in the Bateau-Lavoir were not exactly welcoming to Modigliani. He didn't belong to the Fauvists, the Cubists or the Futurists. Picasso was never his friend. The Spaniard was jealous of his charisma and success with women.

Montmartre and its atmosphere appealed to him – not so much the artistic activity but the mystery. The rue Lepic had always been secretive. Fortunes were told, spells cast, forbidden sexual practices made available. New movements in philosophy were born there. For centuries Montmartre was a huge convent with vine-covered slopes. Ignatius Loyola founded the Jesuit Order, many of whose members were beheaded. The rue des Martyrs, the place des Abbesses marked out the religious territory. In the late 1890s Pigalle, at the bottom of the rue Lepic, became a pleasure ground with spectacular, louche nightlife.

In 1909 Modigliani moved in destitution to Montparnasse and lived at various addresses, all temporary. He worked with the sculptor Brancusi who, like him, believed that sculpture as an art form was dying. Rodin and others debased it by turning it into modelling. The only salvation lay in carving directly from stone. After a quarrel Modigliani left Brancusi and went home to work in Livorno for a while. Back in Paris his drinking was phenomenal, his health declining. Emanuele wanted him to return home. In 1912 he put all his energy into sculpting and exhibited seven heads without success. Jacques Lipchitz, the Russian sculptor who loved the younger Modigliani, remembered how lovingly he worked on them: 'I can see him now, leaning over those heads. He explained they formed an ensemble. He placed them in the exhibition at the Salon d'Automne, placed together like the pipes of an organ to express the music that sang in his soul.'

Jacob Epstein said he lit a candle on top of each head at night and you thought you were in an old temple. Stoned on hash, he kissed the statues.

Ossip Zadkine visited him in 1913:

I found him lying on a tiny narrow bed. His magnificent velvet suit floated on a turbulent sea, frozen till he woke up. White sheets of paper were everywhere, on the walls and on the floor, covered with drawings, like crests of waves from a storm in a silent film, motionless for a moment. He who was so beautiful and delicate with his oval face, woke up unrecognisable, yellow-skinned and drawn. The goddess hash spares no one.

Zadkine, a sculptor and Russian Jew, was a calm, sober, resourceful man who saw his mission as one to revive Jewish sculpture.

After a terrible winter, Modigliani's health obliged him to return home. His work was scorned; he tipped his sculptures into a Livorno canal, and fled back to Paris. He continued his sculpture but finally saw he didn't have the strength, the health or the money for the materials. He gave up in 1913 and it was as though something died inside him.

Jean Cocteau wrote of Modigliani:

At Montparnasse, we could afford the luxury of being poor. Poverty was something gay, something we should find impossible today; much too expensive. The result is that we are now showing our dear Modigliani in fancy dress; but this theatrical character has nothing to do with his painting.

He was always proud and rich, when we knew him; rich in the real sense, drawing the elongated portraits of his friends and wandering from table to table at the Café de la Rotonde like a fortune-teller

Was he handsome? I have been wondering since I saw Gérard Philipe portray him in a film. No. He was something better. And he greeted mockery with his terrible laughter . . .

He was like those models in Rome who at one time waited for painters on the Spanish steps. His hair was short and curly, his beard [which would have been a thick one] darkened his hollow cheeks. A dark fire lit his whole being and passed ever into his clothes, to give even their negligence a dandified air. He was gay, witty, charming; and as none of us ever had the least notion of success, he lived royally in the glory bestowed on him by our group, for whom commercial values and the problem of the general public did not exist.

Cocteau tried to help Modigliani. The help was not accepted. Modigliani hated pity. Cocteau says their life was 'simple and violent in those days. Modi epitomised it. He drank of course. But then who didn't?'

Indenbaum said, 'He was wonderful with his handsome head, the gentleness of his face and such intelligence in the expression of his eyes.'

His work was not receiving the success it deserved, and he knew it. He had to fight illness, addiction, bitterness, rejection and poverty. He was now well on the way towards dying of tuberculosis. The success he knew he should have was bestowed on lesser artists. He knew he was doomed – and this was the man who so desperately wanted to prove himself and be recognised. Even dying, he couldn't bear to go home to his mother a failure.

The dealer Chéron took him on, unsuccessfully. Then Paul Guillaume took over, and this partnership seemed more promising. He had a certain influence on Modigliani, but could do little with his work because it wasn't French. He tried to encourage him to paint 'French'. Perhaps in retaliation Modigliani painted Guillaume with a smug and languid expression. In 1914 Modigliani lived for a short while with Diego Rivera, then began his first serious affair.

He was thirty and she a few years older – cultured, sharp, independent and very jealous: Beatrice Hastings, the South African writer, friend of Katherine Mansfield, wrote for the English magazine *New Age*. She was New Age in her style and wanted to be on the pulse of the time, setting trends. Modigliani and Beatrice were well suited intellectually and alcoholically. They provided the art communities with some startling scenarios. On one occasion he threw her through a window – he hadn't bothered to open it first. Her money allowed them a certain style and a lot of drink during their tempestuous affair. He painted regularly for Guillaume, but there were few sales.

Modigliani left Beatrice in 1916, left Guillaume too, and moved to another temporary address. His health was cracking up, his life now dependent on alcohol. Simone Thiroux became his mistress and Leopold Zborowski his dealer. Zborowski was Polish and had come to Paris in 1913. He had a black moustache and beard and a serious air. He had a sales knack and was sensitive to art, and was described as patient and gentle when dealing with Modigliani. The Sitwells thought he was kind, soft, with an air of melancholy. But they weren't fooled. They also knew he was a businessman.

Modigliani had some work exhibited in La Salle Huyghens, one of the avant-garde centres in Paris. He was a merciless, sarcastic mimic. He hid his bitterness. He was still beautiful. Max Jacob described him as

Quite small with curly hair. [He was five foot five inches but held himself well.] A flat profile but beautiful, a pale rather round face, a short but ringing bitter and childlike laugh. He was upright, compact, his violence was unexpected coming with his apparent gentleness, emotional despite his stiffness and tempers, seeming more sardonic than he really was. He was a poet and an artist through and through. He only thought about art.

Lipchitz, who made his death mask, said, 'It's obvious why women were so mad about him. He was so beautiful even in death.'

Cocteau said, 'He was good-looking. No, he was better than that. He had glory.' Then Modigliani met Jeanne.

Chapter Three

Jeanne had seen Modigliani at the artists' carnivals, in the bars, in the streets. He was always noticeable. He would dance in front of the Balzac statue in the boulevard Raspail, round the corner from the Rotonde. He had a wild spent flaring gaiety. On some occasions his friends insisted he go home. He was too drunk. And someone grabbed at his belt but it turned into a long scarlet sash and Modigliani twirled and spun himself along its entire length, off free, into the dark laughing.

He could be spitefully drunk then sober, fastidious and charming within one afternoon. He had style, wit, beauty, intelligence, education. He loved books and poetry. He brought beauty into the room. He gave joy. Both women and men were mad about him. He had a wonderful innocence and delight in life that no amount of disillusion and bitterness could harden.

Jeanne – intelligent yet sometimes passive; submissive yet sometimes wild – saw him, wanted him, but had to wait. He was then involved with the Canadian Simone Thiroux. Then it was discovered that Simone was expecting a baby, to be born in May 1917. Modigliani said from the first that it could not be his. He'd caught her in bed with a close friend. Simone was desperately in love with Modigliani. It was a Montparnasse scandal.

Georges Charaire, who paints today in the studio below Modigliani's, says, 'Everyone lived as though the next minute wouldn't come. They'd been through the war, don't forget. Death was usual.' Georges was born round the corner from the rue de la Grande Chaumière and has lived in the *quartier* all his life. He knew Modigliani but hastens to say that he was only a boy at the time. His father and the studio landlord told him plenty of stories.

According to Germaine, her friend had been in love with Modigliani before she became involved with him. She'd known him for some time before he asked her to sit for him in spring 1917. Their affair began around that time, the month of the artists' carnival. The notebook describing her feelings when seeing him was found by André in her old bedroom after her death. He cleaned the room and gave the notebook to Germaine, who couldn't bear to look at it. It remained among her possessions until after her death. It contains Jeanne's thoughts, anguish, longing, excitement and some everyday anecdotes. On every page there are small drawings, over the actual handwriting.

Before the war, when Jeanne was in her mid teens, she and Germaine talked about the affairs of the *quartier*. On Fridays at 8 p.m. Paul Fort, the prince of poets, gave readings at the Closerie des Lilas. Outside the Closerie there was a street fair and artists stayed up all night, every night. Every two or three weeks a dance was held in a café on the avenue du Maine. Everyone went in fancy dress. And there were the Marie Wassilieff parties. How outside it all they felt! They couldn't wait to grow up. They'd been able to get to the Gaieté Montparnasse, a music hall presenting funny, vulgar revues. They heard about the soirées given by the Baroness Oettingen, a wealthy Polish woman, keen on the arts, who lived in the boulevard Raspail.

The Académie Colarossi was giving its annual fancy-dress ball. The girls planned what to wear. André had told Jeanne how after the Rotonde closed at 2 a.m. the regulars went on to the all-night cafés in the boulevard St Michel. Some of the artists never seemed to sleep.

In the late winter/early spring of 1917 Jeanne would leave her parents' apartment in the rue Amyot and walk past the Panthéon to her class in Montparnasse. She was eighteen and she had the feeling that something important and wonderful was about to happen. She wanted to leave home and go to unknown destinations, to be an adventurer. Like Germaine, she wanted to be free. The chilly bright mornings provoked a sharp sense of anticipation. She'd got through the usual quick breakfast in the kitchen with her parents. How she hated the hot milk! The sight of it being poured into the jug! Her father insisted it should be very hot. Moreover, he wanted to know what she was doing and when she would be home. She was now a woman and should be watched.

Jeanne loved the flowers, their brightness in the stalls by the Rotonde. Across those early-spring blooms she could see, on the terrace of the café, Modigliani in his corduroy suit and red scarf – a charismatic figure, elegant whatever he wore. And she loved him too.

Yet she was not a personality of Montparnasse. She was still an observer, young, yet somehow resolved: an old soul. Foujita used to see her in the Rotonde after her class. She'd already shown him her drawings. Modigliani had seen them too, and she'd seen his. Sometimes they were strangely alike. Germaine said on occasion she could not authenticate a Modigliani because she'd seen Jeanne doing it. And the forger Elmyr de Hory mistakenly copied Jeanne, thinking it was Modigliani.

In 1917 Modigliani was with his final and most suitable dealer, the Polish poet Zborowski, who furnished him with a model, a hotel room and enough drink to get him through the session. Modigliani liked to get it done in one go. Great intensity and energy were necessary. Drink gave fuel. He got through a bottle of spirits in an hour. Otherwise he sketched the café clients: five francs a sketch, never more. He'd fling the sketch down with contempt if the sitter tried to give him extra. He wasn't one of the big names. He wasn't Picasso. He wasn't lucky like Kisling. Like Soutine, Kisling was the son of a tailor, but wealthier. He was an extrovert, loved painting and having a good time. He adored extravagant parties and magnificent gestures. He received a regular allowance from home, and inherited money from the American sculptor Chapman Chandler who was killed in action. Kisling attracted money, even from people who hardly knew him. Whereas Modligiani's genius wasn't only unnoticed, in some cases it was reviled. How he suffered from the Parisian rejection, seeing those with less talent getting acclaim. The money didn't matter. He never paid much heed to money. He'd put himself through every kind of test of deprivation and passed. Modigliani was now in a new phase of his life. This was the epoch of his great nudes. The patient, devoted Zborowski, although impoverished himself, managed to scrape a few francs together to give his client regular support.

Jeanne wasn't like the artists Modigliani knew, who frequented the cafés. She had a home, security, acceptance. The artists he knew lived from hand to mouth, usually with only a drink in their hand. They went hungry, but there was companionship in hunger. Georges

Charaire remembers that time: 'We didn't have money for coal. We made our own warmth.'

Jeanne adored his drawings – but more, she adored him. He was what she'd been seeking, the lover she'd longed for.

Foujita certainly liked her. According to André Salmon she did spend some time with the Japanese painter, but it was only a dalliance. According to Foujita himself, however, it was a little more serious and lasted a month. Foujita said Jeanne was *viceuse* (given to vice), sensual, sickly, pale, thin, mysterious, looked like a student. Whether or not their dalliance was consummated, she left him for Modigliani who, Foujita says, never knew about the attraction, and as he was sincere about the girl, Foujita never told him. It was certain that Modigliani did know. If André Salmon knew, everyone knew. There were no unpleasant reverberations, because Foujita went with Jeanne and Modigliani and the group to the South of France the following year.

First Modigliani drew Jeanne, then he took her to a shabby hotel and painted her. Then he slept with her. It certainly happened before 17 May, when she describes going to the Hôtel Dieu and having her underclothes torn. She had to sew them up. 'A night not without a certain horror,' she told Germaine. Then on 17 June she wrote from the Hôtel Evanquer in the rue Raine, room number 47, where she had been sleeping with Modigliani. It was three o'clock in the afternoon and she did not regret what she had done.

She became his mistress and his friend. She was nineteen. Her hairstyle changed, so did her handwriting. Sexuality and adoration, aided by alcohol, tipped it across the page in large wild symbols. Germaine knew. André knew. Her parents knew nothing. Every night she went home to the rue Amyot. Often the painter Mondzain saw Modigliani walking with her, his arm around her like a lover. He did not, however, go as far as the front door. Modigliani was not suitable – he was penniless, a drunk, a failure, a Jew. His paintings – you couldn't have given them away. He was thirty-four, took drugs, mixed with outcasts like Soutine and Utrillo. Surprisingly, he had grace and was educated. Surprisingly, he was beautifully mannered. He had something about him, but not for the Hébuternes' daughter.

She could not hide ecstasy. Unhappiness, yes. Disapproval, even anger. Her parents saw she was changed. Inquiries were made. They didn't like what they heard. André, according to Germaine, tried to reason with Jeanne. Her parents used argument to try to make her give him up, then they used religion, then they threw her out. They never expected she would actually go. They believed the years they'd given her of spiritual righteousness and moral guidance were a strong enough example, a severe enough weapon against the godless Italian. They hadn't counted on her passion or her wildness. The affinity she experienced with her lover. Germaine was approached to try and make her friend see sense. Then Madame Hébuterne pleaded with her daughter. Monsieur Hébuterne took solace in the local church. His priest advised him. He even reasoned with the wayward girl.

Jeanne kept a cool front. She didn't pass on her distress to her lover. She didn't want to put him off. If he'd known how bad it was, that rupture at home, he might have encouraged her to go back. She was young, and she now had no means of support.

Chana Orloff was surprised to hear that Jeanne had left her family 'to follow Modigliani'. More worldly than Jeanne, she saw him in a different light. She counted the drinks and the women.

André witnessed a much-quoted scene by the Luxembourg Gardens. Hearing an angry, drunken snarl he ran forward and saw Modigliani raging and attacking Jeanne. He pushed her into the railings, pulling her plaits. Salmon called for him to stop. Jeanne ran away, but not from her lover. The multitude of rats that came up from the drains at that time of night made her panic. Modigliani caught up with her and they 'vanished into the night', as was Modigliani's custom.

Madame Hébuterne believed this crisis was a moral test sent by God. It was her duty not to let Jeanne go. Prayer and constant visits would bring the straying lamb back. But it was hard to find Jeanne, for she was closeted away in the warren of tawdry hotels Modigliani used.

One afternoon, accompanied by Madame Diriks, wife of Dr Diriks, Simone Thiroux appeared. Her son Gérard had been born. She had a private meeting with Modigliani in the Hôtel des Mines. He refused to acknowledge paternity. She left desperate, not seeing Jeanne waiting in the corridor. According to Madame Diriks, Simone immediately went to call on another man, with no success there either. No one in Montparnasse had any real doubt that the child was Modigliani's – except Modigliani.

Simone Thiroux was fun-loving, a careless Bohemian, half-model, half-artist, living for the moment. She danced, laughed, liked a good time. She was crazy about art. She was blue-eyed, blonde, well built, with a bosom she was proud of and liked to show off on every occasion. At one time she had inherited money which she threw away, gave away, disposed of pleasurably. She'd been brought up in Canada and now lived with her aunt in the rue Huysmans. However, the tide of good fortune had turned on this happy-go-lucky girl. Her passion for Modigliani halted her carefree days. Her money was gone, she had a baby and her aunt had now thrown her out. Finally, the man she adored was not only denying paternity but also said he never wanted to see her again.

Jeanne certainly witnessed Modigliani's dramatic response to Simone. He couldn't even bear to have her name mentioned. His behaviour displeased many in Montparnasse. Simone did not deserve such treatment. Dr Diriks and his wife Marguerite helped her. So did Fritz Sandahl, a Swede who'd lived in Montparnasse since 1911.

Simone would certainly have been one of the café personalities Jeanne and her friends watched, envied and criticised. A woman of the world, she bestowed money and affection on those she liked. She put on a splendid display of living, with no sense of consequences, adorning and glorifying 'the now', with her freshly acquired clothes. She never bothered to wash anything, just threw it away and bought something new. Jeanne must have heard of the fight in the Rotonde when Beatrice Hastings came calling and saw Modigliani with Simone. He had seen Beatrice with a younger lover. He was provocative, with his merciless laugh. Beatrice hurled a glass at his head. It caught Simone over the eye, leaving a scar. Libion, the proprietor, threw them out. There was a furious quarrel.

Now it was Jeanne's turn. She could see that the Canadian had much in common with Modigliani. She too was tubercular and cared little about her health. Like him, she used herself up. Like him, she was well educated. She'd taken a degree before coming to Paris, and for a while she'd studied at the Sorbonne. Unlike Beatrice, Simone did not attack her rival. Jeanne did, so it was reported. She slapped

Simone's face hard when she showed up at the hospital while Modigliani was dying.

According to the Diriks and Fritz Sandahl, Simone never could get over him and tried repeatedly to get him back. Jeanne, however, was confident of his feelings for her – but she was also alert. There was always the possibility that he might again desire that other, voluptuous, different sort of woman.

Chapter Four

The summer of 1917 was a happy time for Jeanne. She'd got the man she loved. She was drawing and painting and also modelling for him. She was now his companion in the cafés, wearing the exotic clothes he liked. She sat listening as he talked to Picasso, Ehrenburg, Kisling, Salmon, Ortiz de Zárate and other companions. She was present when he debated landscape with Diego Rivera: 'Landscape? Don't make me laugh – it does not exist.' Modigliani painted only two landscapes in his life, and then only because he couldn't find anyone to paint. Jeanne was now a café star. During this time Indenbaum described her as 'closed but at the same time very open. She seemed to be contemplating an interior world. Modi was everything to Jeanne: father, brother, husband, fiancé.' Indenbaum felt strongly that the lovers were destined to be together: 'Jeanne was the one person somehow made to love Modigliani. She could understand him. She could feel for him to quite a special degree.'

Dr Diriks said that Jeanne was no beauty, but in his view she had an unusual, interesting face. He found her intelligent, reserved, and thought she did not make friends easily. She had a strong personality.

Fritz Sandahl found her 'strange, with a queer, almost mystic expression in her brooding eyes . . . She talked little and never smiled . . . her lack of gaiety and her silence were the result of her life with the unsympathetic, narrow bourgeois family.' His statement 'she was driven inwards, repressed to the point of perpetual melancholy' seems overdone, but all this was said after her suicide, when she was seen through the veil of death. They had to find reasons for her tragedy. Someone was to blame. They turned to the Hébuternes. Sandahl, who knew Beatrice Hastings and Simone, believed there was no doubt Modigliani adored her: 'Jeanne was the love of his life and to her he was a god.'

Zborowski was at first cautious. Here was a young girl from a bourgeois Catholic family – pure, prepared for a vastly different kind of life – in the company of one who was perched always on the edge, always at the extreme, almost beyond human comprehension. The drink and the drugs saw to that. On his return from drug-induced euphorias he was cultivated, civilised, kind. But increasingly he was frustrated and embittered by his lack of recognition. In his whole life he had only one patron – Dr Alexandre – few commissions and even fewer sales.

Zborowski and his wife Hanka feared for this 'proper' girl. If she'd been a foreigner or had been around a little, it would have been all right. Jeanne being there in his life made them tense. Could she take the Bohemian scenes and revels that flared up when the group got together? Should she be seeing them at all? Modigliani treated her quite formally in public and quite often did not take her to the homes of his friends – out of respect to her.

When it became clear that he was going to stay with her – and also that she seemed to be doing him good – a greatly encouraged Zborowski moved them out of their succession of hotels. He found them a rented studio at the top of a high old building across a courtyard at 8 rue de la Grande Chaumière. The steep, curving wooden stairs taxed the stamina of even the healthy. The hallway floor was tessellated. High above, a skylight let in sun that brought the floor colours to life. The studio was L-shaped: one narrow room at right angles to another which, broken by a passage and the lavatory, became another with a stove in one corner. One wall was comprised entirely of windows, which made the rooms unbearably hot in summer. Hanka had furnished them simply: a wooden table, some chairs that didn't match, and a divan. For light they used a candle or an oil lamp. Modigliani painted the walls in orange, red and yellow as background for his models. They moved their bed from room to room depending on the weather. In the summer they slept in the room furthest from the window, which was shaded in the morning; in the winter, near the stove.

This was a good time – optimistic, sunny, when all the pleasant things of life seemed to come to Jeanne. For a while she was so happy she felt blessed. That terrible step of leaving her parents seemed so far away it could have been in the Dark Ages. Now she was free and able to be herself.

Modigliani liked her simplicity and lack of airs and wiles. Yet for him there were two obstacles to this closeness: his art, for which he

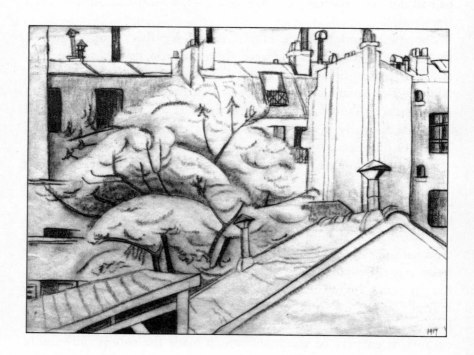

needed to be free, and his mother. The bond with his mother precluded a close domestic relationship with anyone. Therefore Jeanne was discouraged from homemaking. The studio was a place for work. He continued his life as he always had, going out with his drinking companions and eating at Rosalie's or Zborowski's flat in the nearby rue Joseph Bara. And although he could have painted in the studio he did most of his work, especially the nudes, at the Zborowskis'.

Jeanne certainly had time alone, but it didn't seem lonely. She drew Germaine – now with Roger Wild, whom she later married – and sketched aspects of the studio. She also did an oil of the tree in the courtyard below, which was later given to her daughter.

Her letters show that she was clear about her states of being. She could define her moods even if she didn't like them. She was very open about women and men, used to drawing from life. Nudity caused her no embarrassment. She was not inhibited about sex. Her openness and her irony pleased Modigliani. She had a natural mysterious quality which he found tantalising. The others, the aroused ones, were not companions and friends. They registered on the sexual, sensual scale and were magnificent on canvas and possibly in bed. Jeanne could understand ideas that interested him and she wasn't as intellectually cruel as Beatrice Hastings. She joined the series of respected women who posed on chairs – dressed: Lunia, Hanka, and others.

When Modigliani brought someone in to pose, Jeanne went off to the furthest room. He could not bear interruption. She wrote letters and made clothes. In spite of wartime shortages she was able to obtain colourful, even unusual materials. She played the violin, sketched him as he read by oil lamp, in bed or elegant in a hat at the table. She was affectionate, loyal and open to Germaine. There was no reason why she should be different with him. So far life hadn't required her to be defensive with those she approved of and loved. She didn't need to play games to keep him. If this was paradise, there had to be a snake. Jeanne gave it a name: Lunia Czechowska.

In the summer of 1916 Lunia saw her friend Zborowski overwhelmed and excited by someone called Modigliani. He'd seen an exhibition containing some of his paintings and was so obsessed by them that he forced himself to get extra money. He wanted to give canvas and paints to the Italian so that he could paint properly and not have to sketch on café terraces. Zborowski, a keen poker player, tried to get some of the paint money by luck. His obsession with Modigliani meant he had no time to write any more poetry. 'That', said Lunia, 'is how Zbo became an art dealer.'

He took Lunia and her husband to see the exhibition in the rue Huyghens studio, where Modigliani had some work on display. Afterwards, as they sat with friends on the Rotonde terrace, Lunia saw, crossing the boulevard Montparnasse, a very handsome young man wearing a big felt hat, a velvet suit and a red scarf. Pencils stuck out of his pocket and he carried under his arm a big sheaf of drawings. Unerringly he sat next to the lovely Lunia. She wrote that she was taken 'by his distinction, his radiance and the beauty of his eyes. He was at the same time very simple and very noble. How different he was in his least gestures, even to his way of shaking your hand.'

Lunia always insisted that theirs was an exalted, spiritual relationship. When challenged, she said that only their souls were involved, but then Lunia took a proud stance, as she didn't end up with him. During their first meeting, Modigliani sketched her as they talked. She was almost terrified when, in front of her husband – a Polish pastry cook, about to be sent to the Front – he asked her to go out with him that evening. He seemed to expect that she would respond openly to what they both obviously felt: 'Poor dear friend. What seemed so natural to him was so outlandish to me.' Modigliani knew she was attracted to him and wanted her. What did he care about husbands? It was June 1916 and the next day he began a series of paintings, some of which were actually sold in his lifetime. She was a lucky model for him and the subject of some of his best work.

And now, in summer 1917, Lunia came to the studio eager to help, to talk and bring him flowers. Jeanne sensed a rival. He'd be aroused and quite eager for the conquest Lunia was proposing without seeming to, over a bowl of flowers or fruit. There always seemed to be people at the door, taking him away.

Jeanne went with Modigliani to one of the most exciting Montparnasse events of 1917: Kisling's wedding. A riotous, high-spirited affair, everyone behaving as Bohemians were expected to. Kisling, *en grand seigneur*, led his party from the Rotonde to a grand dinner in Leduc's restaurant. Chana Orloff said:

> In the midst of the meal when Kisling was sufficiently ripe, he told his guests, 'I shall dance the dance of chastity.' He pulled his shirt out of his trousers and he galloped around us; after which he declared, 'You take care of the bill,' and he skipped. There was a moment of stupefaction, then a general 'every man for himself'. But the *patron* was at the door with a policeman. How we got out I don't know but we felt no resentment toward Kisling and we went to his place to continue the celebration.
>
> What follows is unbelievable to relate. The drunks were making a frightful racket on the stairs and a sculptor amused himself tearing up a collection of Kisling's drawings and scattered them down on the head of the *concierge*. Kisling, at the highest pitch of rage and aided by several of his companions, managed to throw the sculptor down the stairwell from the seventh story. But miraculously he clutched and clung as he went, and he survived. To the present day he has a searing recollection of his flight. Once more two policemen were waiting at the door when we came out.

The second event after Kisling's marriage was the opening of the ballet *Parade* with music by Erik Satie, story by Jean Cocteau and costumes and sets by Picasso. It was held at the Châtelet Theatre: '. . . the huge auditorium was packed to bursting and with a turbulent audience, out to make trouble'.

The writer Michel George-Michel says the whole of Montparnasse was in a state of high excitement:

> All the painters came and stood about in their sweaters and working clothes, pushing their way among the fashionable ladies

63

in the boxes. There were the most extraordinary combinations of people, some of the most picturesque of them in the Director's box, presided over by Missa Edwards in black and white satin with Picasso wearing his customary jockey's cap and garnet red pullover. In the box where I was there were half a dozen painters from the 'Cubist' cafés and among them the melancholy Noix de Coco, Modigliani's fiancée, Mlle Hébuterne, the Citron sisters, Hélène Perdriat, Lagar, Ortiz de Zárate and two actresses from the Comédie Française . . .

Modigliani did not take Jeanne to the third event of 1917, the banquet given for Fernand Léger and Georges Braque returned from the war. It was held at Marie Wassilieff's canteen and she was scrupulous about the guest list. She didn't want trouble and bribed Modigliani to stay away. His ex-mistress Beatrice was coming with her new lover, Pina. Picasso had his doubts that everything would go smoothly, and he was right. Marie Wassilieff recounts how, at the end of the meal, 'the doors burst open and there was a whole band of painters and models who hadn't been invited. Pina, when he saw Modigliani, drew a revolver and pointed it at him. I seized the gun by main strength, forced him out of the door and he rolled down the stairs.'

The party was the kind Kisling approved of: 'By six in the morning Braque and Derain were dancing with the bones of the lamb.'

Chapter Five

By September, Jeanne was back in Brittany. It would seem that her mother and prayer had won. She was trapped there, looking over at the sea she adored, but numb, without feeling. It was clear that she was ill:

> Despite the atmosphere I am completely empty. I am emptied of all mysticism and calmness. I long for Montparnasse. Nothing doing. All this beauty here bores me and makes me angry. I can look out at the Breton roofs with the little tree growing beside them but all I can think of is going back to Paris. I am sorry about my mentality and my physical state with its headaches, loss of appetite, bad sleep – hardly sleep. Ridiculous symptoms but I've got to admit them. I feel dreadful about lost hope of being able to feel good anywhere. I can hardly paint. My prayer would be to go off to an unknown destination. I struggle and I still haven't heard any news, which is the last straw. My anguish . . . and here I'm having the calmest life possible with no stimulants from the outside so it's all coming from myself . . . But I'm writing what is impossible to write. There you are . . .

The news she was waiting for hadn't come because Modigliani hadn't written a letter. Their relationship, with its consequences, had to be weighed up. There is no doubt he took it seriously and it is the first time he stirred himself to do something about a woman. She was his responsibility. Beatrice had kept him. It's unlikely he'd kept Simone. Jeanne was his first taste of commitment. It wasn't just a question of whether she could live without him, but could he live without her?

Jeanne had been ill before and mentions suffering from headaches. In the late summer of 1917 she'd started to become unwell again and her mother, hearing about it, saw that God had answered her prayers. She took her in hand, away from the evil attractions of Montparnasse. Because she no longer lived at home and had no money Jeanne was not looking after herself properly. Modigliani, an alcoholic, wasn't too fussed about eating. Jeanne was happy, but happiness did not fill the stomach.

There were rumours that she'd been pregnant and lost the baby in the early months, either by design or naturally. The studio, up many flights of stairs, was no place to be ill. How could she get help? There wasn't a telephone. Immediately below, in the studio previously occupied by Gauguin, Ortiz de Zárate lived with his wife and family. Although he was a friend of Modigliani's and had known him years ago in Italy and liked to drink and take drugs with him, his wife Hedwige deplored the state in which he returned after a few hours with the Italian. Not only did she ban Modigliani from her home, she would not have him or his lifestyle mentioned in front of their child. It didn't seem to Jeanne that their neighbours would be of help. She could hardly go back to her parents' home. So her mother put her in the place which suited her best. At the end of the letter to Germaine she states, 'Help! My mother is determined to leave me here till the end of the month, but I rot away here.'

It's unlikely she stayed till the end of the month, or even to the end of her malaise. Life was where he was. Without him there was no point to anything. Already she saw the trap – with him, the light was on. Without, darkness.

Back in Paris a time of hope was beginning: Modigliani was to have his first one-man show in December. Madame Hébuterne would have preferred her daughter to return home. She was a strong woman and could placate her husband. But Jeanne went unerringly to her lover. Madame Hébuterne gave her an ultimatum: no more sexual practices outside wedlock. It wasn't a question of offending her father, but the sanctity of the Church. A bastard child could not be recognised by the true faith. Outside Catholicism nothing else existed. Jeanne could understand her mother's ardent religious feelings. They were not dissimilar from those she had for Modigliani.

There was little contraception for women in those days except washing afterwards and, if possible, peeing immediately: old wives' tales that didn't work. Some girls used a sponge like a diaphragm; others used coitus interruptus, called 'taking care'. Modigliani was not always sober enough for that.

Now he was involved with her family. They demanded a meeting.

He said he was sincere about Jeanne, but he disliked the conventional manmade laws designed to protect the frightened bourgeois, and he would not kowtow to the Hébuternes' 'little gods'. He found their beliefs and way of expressing them laughable; their lifestyle stultifying. No wonder André and Jeanne had escaped. His attitude had not changed since he'd written to his friend, the artist Oscar Ghiglia, in Italy in his teens: artists are beyond normal morality. It was an attitude Jeanne could embrace. It took care of the relentless doubts about defying God, the question of sin, her guilt for causing her parents such anger and distress.

Jeanne was entranced by Bohemian life. Once in the cafés she could cast off her bourgeois trappings. To some degree she drank with Modigliani, but she could always get him home. On occasion she needed help. The painter André Durey got him up the stairs and on to the bed. Modigliani sobered up almost immediately and began reading a book, quite peacefully. Jeanne thanked Durey and at that moment Modigliani leapt up and began smashing everything in sight in sudden rage, shouting how he hated the war. It took both of them some time to restrain him. Sometimes Ortiz would carry him back from the Rotonde and up the huge flights of stairs. Ortiz was large, with big hands. In the winter he carried up their coal, and water from the tap in the courtyard.

This helpless drunkenness was only one side of Modigliani. He could change very quickly and become sunny and full of life, self-determining, precise, clever and undeniably attractive. When Jeanne returned from Brittany she went straight to the studio in the Grande Chaumière. She opened the door: he was working. He was full of energy, almost radiant. Plainly this was where she belonged. Between one day and the next he could be transformed. Jeanne scrawled a note on a small drawing she sent to Germaine, testifying to her happiness. It was as though their souls had made a pact long before their bodies came into being. When he saw Jeanne his eyes brightened. She was unique. In his fashion he loved her. One difference – he could live without her.

Chapter Six

Modigliani had written his five letters to Oscar Ghiglia at the age of seventeen. Ghiglia, a fellow art student in Livorno, had well-developed ideas on art, women, philosophy and spiritualism. At the time he was enjoying artistic success, and Modigliani looked up to him.

The letters were written at various stages of Modigliani's recuperative trip to the South with his mother – his tour of the art masterpieces he had only heard of and longed to see. Although they are quite different from Jeanne's in style and texture, these letters express some of the same themes, and are confiding in a similar way:

... I am here at Capri and I'm taking a cure ... It's four months now since I've accomplished anything but I am accumulating material. I'm going to Rome soon, then to Venice for the Exhibition ... I'm doing just like the English. But the time will come when I'll undoubtedly set myself up in Florence to work, but in the full meaning of the word: that is, to dedicate myself faithfully (body and soul) to the organisation and development of every impression, of every germ of an idea that I have collected in this place as if in a mystic garden ...

Dear Oscar,

Still at Capri. I would rather have waited to write to you from Rome: I'll leave in two or three days but the need to gossip a bit with you makes me take up my pen.

I can well believe that you must have changed under the influence of Florence. Would you believe that I have changed in travelling here? Capri, whose name alone is enough to arouse a tumult of beautiful images and ancient voluptuousness in my spirit, appears to me now as essentially a springlike place. There is – to my way of thinking – a vague feeling of sensuality which is always present in the classic beauty of the countryside ... I went off alone for a country walk in the moonlight with a Norwegian girl ... really a very erotic type but very lovely too ... How is Vinzio? He had started well on his little picture. Is he progressing or dragging his feet? Answer me. That's really why I write, *to have news of you* and the others ...

Dear Friend,

I write to open my heart to you and to confirm my own feelings regarding myself.

I am myself the plaything of strong forces that are born and die in me.

I would like my life to be a fertile stream flowing joyfully over the ground. From now on you are the one to whom I can say everything; well, I am rich and fruitful with ideas now and I need to *work*.

I'm terribly excited, but it's the kind of excitement that precedes happiness and is followed by a dizzy round of activity uninterrupted by thought.

Already, after writing this, I think *it is good* to be so excited. And I'll rid myself of it by plunging again into the great struggle, facing the risks, carrying on the war with a great strength and vision unknown to me until now.

But I must tell you of the new weapons with which I'll again experience the joys of battle.

A bourgeois told me today – he insulted me – that I, or rather my brain, was wasting away. He did me a lot of good. We should all have such a warning every day when we get up; but they don't understand us any more than they can understand life.

But I've told you nothing of Rome. Rome which is not only outside of me but inside of me as I talk. Rome which lies like a setting of terrifying jewels on its seven hills, like seven imperious ideas. Rome is the orchestration with which I surround myself, the limited area in which I isolate myself and concentrate all my thoughts. Its feverish delights, its tragic landscape, its beautiful and harmonious forms – all these things are mine through my thought and my work.

I cannot tell you of all the impressions I've gathered here, nor of all the truths I've found in Rome.

I am going to start a new piece of work but already after blocking and planning it, a thousand other ideas have sprung out of my day-to-day life. You see how important it is to have a method and apply oneself.

Besides, I am trying to formulate as clearly as possible the truths of art and life that I have discovered scattered among the beauties of Rome, and as their inner meaning becomes clear to me I will try to reveal and rearrange their composition – I might almost say their metaphysical architecture – to create my own truth on life, on beauty and on art.

Goodbye, my friend. Tell me about yourself as I've told you about myself. Isn't that the meaning of friendship – to write as one pleases about everything and to reveal each to the other and to ourselves?

Farewell,

    Your Dedo.

But Oscar was a poor letter-writer, and didn't reply. By now Modigliani had spent the winter months with his mother touring Naples, Capri, Amalfi, Rome. He was then setting off with her to Florence and Venice. He was her favourite, her adored one, and she wanted to share his first sight of the great art, to see his reactions, absorb his every thought. She was also possessive about his health. He had to keep to a strict routine, intended for invalids. He'd have much preferred a wilder and freer time in these places. But his mother was educated, intelligent, 'a fine woman, a beautiful matron', and on his side.

Dear Oscar,

You had promised me the diary of your life from the day we last saw each other up to now.

As for me, I have broken my promise because I can't keep a diary. Not only because no important outside event has happened in my life, but because I believe that even the inner experiences of the soul cannot be recorded so long as we are in their power . . . Why don't you write to me? And what are these paintings? I read the description of one of them in an article in the *Corriere*. I cannot yet get around to painting; I am forced to stay in a hotel

70

here so you can understand how impossible it is for me to dedicate myself to painting at the moment. But all the same I am working hard mentally and in contemplating nature ... Now write and send me what you promised. The practice of observing the nature and landscape of the Alps will mark one of the greatest changes in my way of seeing things. I'd like to discuss with you the difference between the work of artists who have lived and communed with nature and the artists of today who find their inspiration in study and want to develop themselves in the great art centres ...

Ghiglia found Modigliani charming, with a certain precocious brilliance. But he didn't think his work would amount to much, neither did he agree with the ideas proposed in Modigliani's final letter to him. Modigliani was stating his own beliefs – deeply held, unquenched for the rest of his life. Undoubtedly Oscar Ghiglia was the most important influence of Modigliani's teens, yet later they quarrelled bitterly.

Dear Oscar,
   I got your letter and I'm terribly sorry I lost the first one which you say you sent to me. I understand your pain and your discouragement – alas, more from the tone of your letter than from what you have put down. I think I've grasped what's happened to you. I've gone through the same thing, and believe me, I feel for you sincerely. I don't know exactly what brought all this on, but I sense that you, with your noble spirit, have suffered a severe depression or else, with your right to happiness and a full life, you wouldn't be so discouraged. I repeat that I really don't know what it's all about, but I feel the best remedy is to send you from here, from my heart which is so strong for the moment, a breath of life. For you were made – and believe me – for a life of happiness and intensity. People like us (if you'll excuse the plural) have different rights, different values than do normal, ordinary people because we have different needs which put us – it has to be said and you must believe it – above their moral standards. Your duty is never to waste yourself in sacrifice. Your *real* duty is to save your dream. Beauty herself makes painful demands, but these nevertheless bring forth the most supreme efforts of the soul.

Every obstacle we overcome means an increase in will-power and provides the vital and progressive renewal of our inspiration. Hold sacred (I say it for your benefit as well as my own) everything that will stimulate and excite your intellect. Try to provoke, to freshen all these stimulating forces which can alone push your intelligence to its maximum creative power. This is what we have to fight for. Can we possibly achieve such goals hemmed in by narrow moral values? Always speak out and keep forging ahead. The man who cannot find new ambitions and even a new person within himself, who is always destined to wrestle with what has remained rotten and decadent in his own personality, is not a man. He is a bourgeois, a grocer, what you will. You could have come to Venice this month but you decide . . . If you want to escape from Livorno I can help you in so far as I can . . .

Modigliani spent the following winter in Rome. He was dressed like an aristocrat and very serious. His friend Ardengo Soffici, painter and writer, said he was a handsome young man with good and gentle features: 'He had a graceful countenance and gracious manners and what he said denoted a great intelligence and a serene frame of mind.' The last time Soffici saw him was in Paris and sadly, he could not help noticing the change. The graceful boy was now a hopeless drunk and drug user. Soffici, like other Italians, made the point that the terrible deterioration happened after he arrived in Paris.

Ortiz de Zárate met Modigliani in Venice in spring 1902. He described him as 'living in comfort, was quite the dandy and as usual was very popular with the ladies'. It was in Venice that he first 'expressed a burning desire to be a sculptor and bewailed the cost of the material. He only used paint *faute de mieux*. His real longing was to work in stone, a longing that remained with him throughout his life . . .'

Ortiz claimed that it was his stories of Paris, the artists' paradise, that so inflamed the Italian that he wanted to leave for France straight away. Ironically, Ortiz was the last to see him alive. Did he remember his inspiring stories as he carried the barely conscious man to the ambulance?

Chapter Seven

To begin with, Zborowski had believed Jeanne would provide the solution to Modigliani's life problems. She would soothe the bitterness of rejection, keep him out of the bars, make sure he ate, and retain a hold on the small sums of money he received. It was a tall order for anyone. If Jeanne had been able to transform an alcoholic into a sober money-saver overnight, no doubt she would have had a queue of people at her door. She'd have been a millionaire. She would have seen that the rise in the alcohol level was a plunge downwards for her and tried to stop him, if only to get the best of the man she loved. It didn't work and she saw that remonstrances were not popular. She shut up. Fortunately, as they had three rooms, she could get out of the way if he was too boisterous. But he seems to have had a strange control while drunk. He could certainly paint. His hand ceased to shake when it picked up a paintbrush. Equally, he didn't abuse everybody, only those he disliked. Neither the landlord's son nor Ortiz remembers any drunken violence towards Jeanne. And Roger Wild said that however drunk he became, he had a respect for her.

Zborowski needed a new infusion of hope. Unable to sell any of Modigliani's pictures, sometimes unable even to give them away, he desperately wanted an event – stimulating, encouraging – something to help his beloved client through this increasing bitterness, sweetened only by drink. His health was failing; they all saw that. The gallery-owner Berthe Weill provided the answer. She agreed to give Modigliani a one-man show from the 3rd to the 30th of December 1917. At last his work would be recognised. Jeanne felt part of this triumph. But it was the Zborowskis, she noticed, who took charge of him during the preparations. It was subtly done, but Jeanne was excluded.

The Zborowskis acknowledged that she sketched well, but in their eyes she was a mere art student. He was the master, and he came first. Moreover, the Zborowskis were snobbish about style. Modi was eminently acceptable because he had breeding and finesse. So did Lunia and Kisling. Jeanne was still young; she had not yet grown into her true style, and around these people she'd learnt to be quiet. Also, she was the daughter of bourgeois – this was incomprehensible. Didn't Modigliani hate the bourgeoisie? They failed to see the true attraction between the Italian and the French girl. It wasn't to do with style, or wit, or even sex. As she wrote, he was a familiar, someone she'd always known. There were similarities between them – small things like the effect of weather. His mother said she could always tell when a storm was coming because he would become quite sarcastic and when it rained he recovered his good humour. And bigger things: their loyalty to people they loved and to his dream – because now hers had become inseparably fused with his. If she wasn't a great artist, she could at least appreciate what he was talking about – the difficulties with sculpture, the mixing of colour, the Italian masters whom he revered, and the fashion of contemporary Paris, which he ignored. He warmed her; in his arms she felt safe. He was hers. But when he was absent, who knew whose he was?

The Zborowskis were too sophisticated to deal with Soutine. Chaim Soutine, friendless and unloved, came from a village near Minsk, where his parents and eleven children lived in a hut. Mostly they were starving. He was considered the dirtiest artist in Montparnasse. Inarticulate, brooding, he loved painting rotting meat. His life was constant poverty and hardship. His one light was Modigliani who encouraged him. He said, 'You may be poor but your heart isn't.' Tapping Soutine's chest, 'In there, riches. That's all that matters.' The Zborowskis found him repellent and he got into their flat only on Modigliani's invitation. Modigliani, who was so fastidious, washing from head to foot daily, changing his clothes, loved Soutine to such a degree that he could actually share a bed or park bench with this unwashed Russian who never changed his clothes and didn't know how to clean his teeth. His adoration for Modigliani was such, said Marevna, that he followed a man for two days because he looked like the Italian. Modigliani gave him his cast-off shirts, which he cherished and wore with pride.

Modigliani did most of his paintings in the Zborowskis' flat. If the model was nude, Zbo found excuses to interrupt. The excuses were reasonable enough. They also gave him the opportunity to glance at the model. These interruptions infuriated Modigliani to the point where he could not work. Lunia chose to keep guard. She stood outside the door to prevent 'the violation of a sanctuary'. If Jeanne did appear, wondering when Modigliani would be free, she was treated in the same manner as Zborowski. She wasn't even allowed to speak. Jeanne had no choice but to go back to the studio or wait in a café. As Modigliani was known to sleep with his models during the period of artistic arousal, Lunia may have been guarding what went on inside the room as much as outside. She might not allow herself to go to his bed, but she made sure no one else did. Jeanne saw this at a glance. It made her uneasy. She also knew he had to paint. That came first. She chose not to make a scene and waited downstairs.

On one occasion, a beautiful blonde girl came to pose. She was the model for the pink nude later bought by one of Modigliani's only admirers, the novelist and critic Francis Carco, who'd had a brief affair with Katherine Mansfield. Zborowski, unable to resist seeing this girl naked, pushed past Lunia and appeared in the room. Modigliani, in the heat of his work, concentration now shattered, shouted wildly at Zborowski, then in a fury slashed at the canvas with a brush. Lunia stopped him ruining the picture. She held him, talked him out of it, at the same time quietening the frightened model. The studio was a hive of sexual jealousy and a certain amount of fear. At any moment Lunia could fall from grace.

Jeanne posed for him constantly; he did twenty-six paintings and numerous line drawings but no known nudes. Biographers believe it was because she was a Catholic and timid, but her letters reveal no timidity. Others believe Modigliani refused to reveal his mistress naked to the world. Jeanne herself drew from the nude and had no constraint about the human body, so the reticence was probably his. His nude models were often his conquests. The painting and the sexual act linked together and he'd catch aspects of sexuality on the canvas. But with Jeanne the conquest was already made.

Modigliani had no reticence either about appearing naked. After a certain amount of drinking, he automatically took off his clothes. As

Nina Hamnett remarked 'Everyone knew exactly when he was going to undress, as he usually attempted to after a certain hour.'

Berthe Weill was a surprising saviour for Modigliani. So far she'd refused even to show one of his paintings in her small shop in the rue Victor-Masse, although she displayed his contemporaries – Utrillo, Pascin, Picasso, Van Dongen, Vlaminck. Apparently there was so little space that she would exhibit pictures by pinning them on a washing line with clothes pegs. She was a small, tough, formally dressed woman. Her perceptions may not have been all they should, because she couldn't decide whether or not Modigliani was an alcoholic. She found him cultured, sensitive and superb-looking, but she'd always politely refused to take him on. The sudden turnabout could have been due to Zborowski's persuasive salesmanship.

The exhibition was held at her new shop, Galerie B. Weill, 50 rue Taitbout, Paris 9ᵉ. The programme cover showed a drawing of a Modigliani nude, a long-haired woman with tilted head, arms curled around her breasts, pubic hair in evidence: 'Exposition de Peintures et de Dessins de Modigliani, du 3 décembre au 30 décembre 1917'. She hung a painting of a nude in the window; that drew a crowd. The show opened and was closed by the police the same day – Modigliani was not exaggerating when he said that fate was against him. The police had objected to the model's pubic hair.

Before Jeanne could reach Modigliani and comfort him, Zborowski was embracing him, then Lunia, Kisling, Soutine, and others. Eventually she had her turn, yet it was obvious that although the others were shocked and disappointed he could stand on his own feet. He reacted to the closure not with violence but with bitterness. The effect was not instant – it darkened inside him like a decaying tooth. He did say that Paris would not wake up and see sense. He knew the value of his work.

The closure did draw attention to Modigliani. What other artists had had such treatment? How lucky Picasso was in contrast! Everything he did turned to gold.

Although the show seemed a disaster, the art critic Claude Roy believed that in one sense it was 'a real success, not merely a *succès d'estime*'. People were intrigued to see these sensational nudes barred by the police. They were curious about the artist. The scandalous talk was good publicity. It certainly reached the Hébuternes and only confirmed their black view of the artist's spiritual worth. Some people tried to comfort him, help him. But Modigliani, with his loathing of pity, began to respond with arrogance.

In January he considered going back to Italy. He'd had enough of Paris. He should never have left that country of sun. How happy his life had been in Venice, at the turn of the century, when he was researching the painting techniques of the old masters. That passionate, glorious work gazing at the art of the fourteenth-century Sienese painters, especially the Venetian Carpaccio – that was where he belonged, back in those days. But this was the twentieth century and Italy had no more use for him than Paris. He remembered that last visit to Livorno, when his sculpture had been received with such contempt and ridicule that he'd tipped the lot into a canal and fled back to Paris. How could he go home a failure when his friends from art school – Romiti, Ghiglia – were doing so well? He couldn't fail. For himself, yes, but not for his mother. She'd believed in him. She'd worked for the money she sent him each month. If she wasn't in his actual sight, he could feel her thoughts. He had to win for her. His father had failed and let her down. She'd shown she was strong and brought up the family by starting her school. He needed one piece of success, then he could go back and face those sneering 'friends'. But could he take Jeanne? He had never presented a woman to his mother, and he had never committed himself to one.

He decided to stay in Paris and Jeanne was relieved. There was another side to the city which didn't reject him – the bars, the haunts, the streets and the drinking friends: Soutine, Utrillo. That life attracted and accepted him. It would also kill him. Jeanne did try to help. He appreciated her gentle approach, then went out and got even more drunk. Upstairs in the studio, he saw her flashes of gaiety. Her genuine smile made her lovely. She unloosed her hair, took off her clothes. She came to him in a way that was almost ritualistic. She was his, a pure canvas to do with as he liked. He'd taught her how to please him and get pleasure herself. He wasn't always in the mood for making love, in spite of what they said about him. Sometimes he wanted to read, think, be peaceful. He was moody, changeable, but then he was the beloved son and had to honour the faith his mother had vested in his talent. Her ideas, too, and wishes for him. The bond was there. No amount of escape in drink had loosed it.

Sometimes the amount of drink and drugs made him too ill even to breathe properly, let alone expend energy in pleasure. And the sheer volume of drink and drugs would on occasion cause impotence.

There were hours in the studio which were peaceful and light, so friendly and harmonious that Jeanne could almost believe they'd always known each other well. It must have been in some other life, because their time together had been short and so invaded by other people. He'd go to buy cigarettes and a chance acquaintance would spot him and he'd be drawn off on discussion of art or looking at a friend's work, drinking, meeting people, partying, and not return until the following day. Their time was short because he was dying. The sign of death was clear. She was young and still unharmed. She could get away. And then he'd come back, sobered, exhausted, sleepless, smelling of drink, in the early-morning winter light. He was haggard and unshaven, but he was still the most beautiful person she'd ever seen. She'd encourage him to sleep, and all thoughts of leaving him dissolved with the anxiety of the night. No one after 'Dedo' would seem even alive.

Chapter Eight

Zborowski came up with another instalment of hope – a trip, a change. They'd go to the South with its wonderful colour, scenery, an inspiration for artists. Didn't the great Renoir live there? And Modigliani's health would improve. Zborowski was patient in adversity and forever hopeful, but even he couldn't revive the dying art market in Paris. Because of the war, no one was buying, whereas in Nice, rich people were escaping the war. Zborowski planned to visit them with a selection of 'Modiglianis'. He knew the area because he'd recovered from an illness there. He described its coast and sea air. He omitted to mention its damp and humidity, disastrous for someone with tuberculosis, but then he wouldn't have noticed it. Modigliani agreed to go, seeing the value of a fresh start. And Renoir was one of the few living painters he admired. How he'd gazed at those paintings, with their optimism and innocence, when he first arrived in Paris. For him, Renoir and Cézanne were the modern masters. Another inducement to go was the incessant bombing of Paris by the huge German gun nicknamed Big Bertha.

Jeanne wanted to go too. Zborowski could see Modigliani wouldn't leave her. But the Hébuternes would object. They would certainly put up some opposition if Zborowski encouraged their daughter to go off with her lover. Zborowski decided he was the right person to speak with them. He could handle people like them; he understood their sensibilities. So did his wife Hanka, who had a good 'aristocratic' appearance and wasn't at war with the bourgeoisie. Together they visited the rue Amyot, and confirmed what the Hébuternes already knew: she was not going to give him up. And he did seem to be in love with her. He looked at her tenderly. In the street he put his arm round her. He may have fought and raged with Beatrice and furiously denied Simone his love, but Jeanne he treated with gentleness. Let's make the best of it, said Zborowski, and Hanka said the trip to the Midi could make all the difference. Modigliani would regain his strength, his work would flourish and the money would pour in. Madame Hébuterne mentioned the future. By that she meant: was 'that man' going to marry her daughter? Zborowski gave them the answer he thought they wanted to hear: he was sure Modigliani would marry Jeanne. It was the wrong answer – the mother sincerely hoped he would not. But if her daughter was intent on going, she, Madame Hébuterne, would go with her. No sacrifice was too great to bring her daughter back to her senses, and to the father she'd lost.

Monsieur Hébuterne could see that Zborowski was gentle but ineffectual. He doubted he'd make much difference in the scheme of disaster. But at least he wasn't drunk. Monsieur Hébuterne could not give the trip his blessing, but with his wife there it would look correct socially and in the eyes of the Church.

It was a suitable time to leave the studio because Modigliani could not pay the rent. The landlord's grandson says he offered two paintings in lieu. The landlord wouldn't accept them. How he regretted it years later! So did the grandson:

If my grandfather had taken even one I wouldn't be standing here now. I'd live in luxury in the South Seas. How he kicked himself. A million times. But they all came to him with the same hard-luck story. No money for rent. And they'd offer paintings. Modigliani did say if you take these two they will treble in price and you won't have to be a landlord. He was wrong. They were worth ten times the price in two years. As soon as he died all his work was valuable. They're worth a fortune now. But how could my grandfather know? The artists all said the same thing: I am a genius. Take my picture and you will be a millionaire. Who should he believe? It was like backing a horse.

The grandfather said Modigliani used to sleep with his models and Jeanne had to put up with it if she wanted to keep him. Perhaps she understood. 'They had Bohemian ideas in those days.'

Jeanne was excited about the journey – at last she'd have him to herself. But the group now extended to include Soutine, Foujita and Fernande Barrey the model, as well as Hanka, Zborowski and the odd one out, Madame Hébuterne. They left in March 1918 by train from the Gare Austerlitz.

Madame Hébuterne had believed it would be a short trip – shorter still if she could get Jeanne to see, as she did, how crazy her attraction for this Italian was. She didn't expect to be away for longer than two months. André was still at the war and Monsieur Hébuterne was about to be reposted. She needed to be back in Paris by June. She had her home, her son and her husband on leave to look after. But then she didn't know Jeanne was pregnant.

Her daughter-in-law, André's wife Georgette, agrees that it was an odd thing for her to go with them in the first place. 'But she had a certain understanding of artists, at least more than Monsieur Hébuterne. She could mix with them.'

This was not the case with Modigliani. They were at each other's throats within moments of arrival. For a start she absolutely refused to let him live with her daughter. Zborowski lodged the group in two villas in Haut-de-Cagnes. Jeanne, her mother and the Zborowskis were in 'Le Pavillon des Trois Sœurs' and the rest in the second, higher up the hill.

The landlord, Papa Curel, has been described as 'a crusty old eccentric who claimed to have known many artists and supposedly understood their ways ... a fanatical musician who played the trumpet.' Papa Curel was Père Curel, a respectable doctor. Angelina, an eighty-seven-year-old Italian woman still living in the village, remembers him. And Modigliani. The doctor owned several properties. He was not the one who played the trumpet, which so disturbed Soutine he had to be moved to yet another villa. The description did fit an old man who owned a chicken yard. It was he, not Curel, who took Soutine's paintings and used them to board up his animal pens. People who still remember him today say he could have been one of the Jacobellis, a large Italian family of impoverished farmers who arrived from Italy in 1911. They stuck together and worked the land. Angelina was one of them, although she arrived earlier with her family. She is adamant that Modigliani's paintings were not included in the henhouse disaster: 'That was another story altogether.'

Modigliani instantly missed the atmosphere of Paris and the fun and liveliness of the bars. He spent time looking for a suitable retreat, finding it at the top of the hill next to the château, a cave with no windows full of Italian peasants and the few resident artists. It was owned by Mademoiselle Rose, and when his money ran out he persuaded her to give him credit. He liked the brawls and notoriety of the bar, and Rose liked him. But she would not accept, in exchange for drink, the drawings of refugees. In *Artists' Quarter* it's described how she 'tore up what she deemed to be "ugly geese with long necks", thereby adding yet one more to the crowd who later tore their hair figuratively on learning how much they had lost.'

Modigliani had been living with Jeanne for several months, and she was used to him. Her mother wasn't: she put into action her interpretation of how the relationship should be. It caused the most terrible rows which became bitter and constant, yet Hanka told Douglas Goldring, one of the earliest biographers, that Modigliani painted in spite of the atmosphere: 'Indeed, he had always worked passionately. Nobody could reproach him on that score. He could complete in a few days a picture that could take most men weeks or months to accomplish.'

Zborowski discovered that Nice was no more receptive to art than Paris. The refugees lived well, ate and drank, but they held on to their money and jewels. Zborowski's group had to live sparsely. Madame Hébuterne had brought some money, so she could provide for herself and her daughter.

Jeanne had conceived shortly before they left Paris. She probably didn't realise, and even if she suspected she couldn't be sure. It could have been put down to a late period caused by the disruption of moving. Left to themselves, Modigliani and Jeanne could have sorted out what they felt about it, what they could do. But Madame Hébuterne saw the signs of a newly pregnant girl, and what began as rows about drunken behaviour and unlawful sexual intercourse in her house became rows about carelessness, sin, an unwanted child, and marriage. Jeanne was trapped between loyalty and respect for her mother and her feelings for Modigliani.

Zborowski was now fearful about Modigliani's will to work. He was painting with a huge rush of energy, almost violent, that left him emptied, exhausted. In Paris he'd go to the Rotonde and close it all off with a few drinks, then he'd go to Jeanne for solace or excitement.

Here he went back to a screeching 'mother-in-law'. It was at this point that Zborowski tentatively suggested that he should leave Jeanne. There were so many other women. Modigliani never had choice about anything much – but about women he certainly did. Modigliani listened to no one. He himself knew the answers. He also knew about the baby. Even if he contemplated an abortion it would not have been possible, not with Madame Hébuterne in residence. Although she had loathed the idea of him as a husband for her daughter, she now needed him. The baby must be born in the sanctity of the Church. Why should this new soul be denied God?

Sober, Modigliani could handle her. He simply charmed her, talked about mystical ideas that interested her, quoted from books he loved and, it was rumoured, even painted her. Seeing him drunk, approaching her daughter, nearly killed her. She turned on Jeanne. She should have the baby in obscurity and give it for adoption, then return to Paris and start her life afresh.

Jeanne did not intervene in their fights, and this is perhaps where Hanka, in retrospect, got the idea that she did not talk. Jeanne would sit, quite placid, on the terrace of the villa. Hanka was surprised that she wasn't active in such adversity. Hanka's maid, Paulette Jourdain, said Jeanne 'never did anything'. She was unlikely to know, as she was working for the Zborowskis, not in Jeanne's studio.

From Le Pavillon des Trois Sœurs there's a good view of the coast and the hillside opposite. Jeanne, sitting in the sun, could see Modigliani walking in the spring light, with his dark clothes and red scarf. She didn't know that the track he was taking led behind some trees to the Jacobellis' rundown house, filled with chickens and animals. Jacobelli was a farmer; his wife cleaned in the village. They had several children. Modigliani was painting the wife.

Emile Lejeune, who lived in Haut-de-Cagnes from time to time, said he was a *grand seigneur*, very elevated and elegant. He wasn't the wretch people made him out to be. Lejeune did not particularly like Modigliani but he felt he had to defend him.

Modigliani got Jeanne to himself when he was painting her. Hanka was playing the chaperone. The worst had happened as far as Hanka was concerned: he was now closely tied into a family that hated him. Who could guess how they would try and change him before they would allow this new baby to be part of his life? She could discern the family man lurking within the Bohemian mould. What would the new responsibilities do to his work? And all that hatred! She could see it in the 'mother-in-law's' eyes. His art needed other soil to flourish. Hanka no doubt knew about Jacobelli's wife, as did most of the village, but she kept quiet. Zborowski, ever the optimist, said: now there's a child he will give up drink.

Modigliani could get very close, so close that he seemed to enter the other person. One of his models said it was a strange experience. As he painted, he looked at you and you felt him enter. He knew the person behind the skin. And afterwards he would stay in the model's thoughts for some time. It was said that he had psychic powers. He certainly drew close to Jeanne during those snatched hours when he was allowed to paint her. He couldn't touch her, but he lifted her with his words and that sudden joyous optimism that sprang out from some still unspoilt part of him. He approved of her, was very moved by her. It was there, in his eyes. Afterwards they walked in the nearby fields and he told her things about life – knowledge given to him by his grandfather, real wisdom, not facts acquired in schools. And he showed Jeanne life's symbols, its signs. He understood its mysticism and the hidden language in the arrangement of sun and shadow in an afternoon street, comprehensible only to those who knew it.

The next day he would be brimming with a black glowering rage. He hated the Mediterranean light. He couldn't paint unless he returned to Paris. He was now accustomed to Northern Europe and the southern light no longer suited his work. And Zborowski couldn't find anyone to sit for him. He did a landscape and later another, and didn't like them. There was no food. Madame Hébuterne shared what little she had. She could not see them starve. Modigliani tried to get credit and failed, so he went to the Jacobellis and brought back a fowl.

Then the short peace was over. Her mother and Modigliani raged more stormily than ever. They were fighting over more than a person: ideas, ideals, God. Their beliefs were strong, and totally opposed. The mother told him to stay away from her daughter. Jeanne was not heard to intervene – she was utterly silenced by this attack. Modigliani told her to go with him. But where? With what? Her mother told her to stay where she was. Jeanne knew nothing about pregnancy, her mother did. Jeanne was small and delicate – none of it was going to be easy. He saw the way her eyes turned automatically to her mother with habitual obedience, and he raced from the house. And her mother saw how Jeanne's eyes followed him, fevered, longing. She thought it was more than longing – it was a gaze nearing rapture, more intense than anything she'd seen even in a church. It was the gaze of someone who'd seen God.

Chapter Nine

Not everyone was having a bad time. Soutine, who'd never seen the sea, was entranced. Foujita said his excitement was 'boundless'. He also found the climate of the Midi overwhelmingly soporific. He spent most of his time lying in the sun waiting for Zborowski to sell one of his pictures and make him rich. Foujita said he looked like a lizard. Like Modigliani, the Japanese tried to clean Soutine up, to teach him to use a knife and fork and clean his teeth. 'Soutine worked in a regular deluge of colour, with newspapers on the floor under him and paint all over his arms,' Foujita said. He watched Modigliani work, and Foujita always remembered his 'orgasmic' behaviour. How this word has stuck! – if he used it at all. Suzy Solidor, the famous model and cabaret queen who lived in Haut-de-Cagnes in her last years, didn't think so. She'd heard from Kisling that he worked in great passion and tumult, but it didn't resemble a sexual experience. Foujita did say, 'He went through all sorts of gesticulations, his shoulders heaved, he panted, he made grimaces and cried out. You couldn't come near.' And Lunia said he painted with such violence, the first time she sat for him, that he terrified her.

Already the rent was in arrears and they'd have starved without the advances paid to Foujita by Chéron and Zamaron. Zborowski had located Renoir, who lived below in Les Collettes, towards Cagnes-sur-Mer. This was perhaps the answer, the new hope. The hotels were arid and exhausting. He was reduced to the performance of a street hawker, accosting clients with canvases.

Modigliani had still not returned. Everyone was sure he was getting drunk in Nice. Jeanne realised her life was mostly waiting, waiting for him to come back. If she went out he wouldn't find her when he did return, and he was all she wanted to see. She thought back to those safe days when she used to write to Germaine and she wrote her one more letter, which she was uncertain about sending. They were not as close now because Modigliani took all Jeanne's concentration. There had been some sort of falling-out. His getting

drunk had something to do with it. But how she needed her confidante now, and missed the easy exchange of gossip. Her mother was no confidante. Jeanne used reason to calm her. She waited until Hanka was out of the house. She made it clear to Madame Hébuterne that she could not leave Modigliani, that the baby would bring joy to both of them, that he was exquisitely talented with a very rare perception. She saw it. So did Zbo and others. In time Paris would; and all this unhappiness and torment would be understood. Madame Hébuterne remained quiet. She was trying to think of the best way to tell Jeanne's father the bad news, or perhaps it would be better to say nothing. She would have to extend her stay. She didn't chastise the girl further because in certain moods Jeanne didn't seem like her daughter. She just wasn't hers any more.

In one of her last letters to Germaine, Jeanne had written: 'You've got a beauty in you, balance and the harmony you've found, and whatever you do or think could never take this beauty away from you.' Whereas Jeanne herself could be riven, shocked, in pieces, furious and ashamed. And it showed, all of it, in her manner and face. She had to keep a very careful control. Sometimes, if it was too bad, her very nature seemed to plant a skin between her and the horror, as though protecting her.

In the old days, when she'd gone dancing and laughed in the cafés, she'd teased Germaine. In one letter she wrote: 'Is it always your intention to stay in Paris? Is it calm in your *quartier*? Don't get bombed.' She'd suggested that Germaine could bring universal events on to her head just by being there. It was to do with her lack of practicality and common sense. Standing in a street, she could bring the one lone bomb out of the sky. But it was a light-hearted teasing because she approved of Germaine and she was always affectionate: 'I send you all my affection and I give your hands a good clasp.' Or she ended a letter with 'I give you a friendly clasp. I am definitely expecting you the day after tomorrow and while waiting I shake your little silk hands warmly.'

Jeanne was always eager to discuss the news of Montparnasse: 'Come then to me, not late. Then we will have time to analyse together what's happening. Soon, my old Bibi. I am in a hurry to see you. Come early. I squeeze your hands strongly . . . Tell me news of the club. And the Chaumière [art school]. Has it reopened? Good-bye, Red Bean. Make again your superb documentary studies [a way of gossiping].

'We'll go for a walk and chatter to our hearts' content.'

She was truthful. After sleeping with Modigliani in a shabby hotel, she wrote, 'I am here completely alone. So alone that I've got no more reason to be. Forgive me but I suffocate and I do not regret that I went to bed or admitting it.'

And when she was ill, 'All the time lately I've been very bored. I have a headache. I can't even do any more work. I did not return to school and, more, I messed up my life drawings.'

Both women loved clothes and Jeanne described her purchases and what she'd made. She wrote about a new dress she was about to try on. 'Blue green, the same as the last but a lot bigger. More puckered with pleats that fall to the ground.'

Underneath her light-heartedness she was quite determined in her efforts to get the practical facts that so bored her friends: 'My dear Bibi, stay agreeable while I give you various practical requests about the place you are staying in because we have *vague* projects to stay in the country. Tell me for example if it's a long trip and if it's

1. A recently discovered photograph of Jeanne from the private collection of her best friend Germaine Labaye showing her more beautiful than usually thought.

2. This photograph of Jeanne caused some biographers of Modigliani to assume she was unattractive. Underneath is a letter Jeanne wrote to Germaine Labaye.

3.   One of three portraits of Jeanne by Modigliani where her eyes are brown instead of blue. Lanthemann, an authority on Modigliani, said the paintings were therefore of another girl, but many have disputed this.

4.   8 bis rue Amyot in Paris where Jeanne lived with her parents and brother André. She left to live with Modigliani, but returned to die here.

5. This photograph comes closest to showing Modigliani's legendary beauty and magnetism.

6. A photograph of Modigliani, unusually unposed – taken shortly before his death in January 1920.

7.   The studio in rue de la Grande Chaumière, Paris, where Jeanne lived with Modigliani. It had uncurtained windows which let the sun in at all hours and seasons. It is virtually unchanged today.

8.   The only known painting by Jeanne Hébuterne. This is the first time it has been publicly shown as the family guarded it closely.

9.   Jeanne standing in front of a mirror.
The drawings pinned on the wall behind
are probably hers.

10.   The much-reproduced drawing by
Jeanne of Modligiani. Her style was so
similar to his that the forger Elmyr de
Hory copied this mistakenly believing it
to be a self-portrait by Modigliani.

11.　The house in Haut-de-Cagnes where Modigliani stayed in 1918. This photograph, taken in the 1950s, shows Ulla Fribrock (centre) who's father-in-law, Emile Lejeune, knew Modigliani and Soutine. Since then the house has been modernised and completely transformed. This is one of the few remaining pictures showing the house as it was in Modigliani's time.

12.　This tram ran between Cagnes and Nice, and Modligiani, Jeanne and her mother used it regularly. In the background is the fortress village of Haut-de-Cagnes.

13.　Lina (far left), Modigliani's illegitimate daughter, with Louise Cornou (far right) and friends (some more friendly than others) in Paris during the Second World War.

14.　Louise Cornou (seated far right), the artists' model and later master chef with Lina (standing) in Haut-de-Cagnes shortly after Louise arrived from Brittany in 1938.

15. A studio portrait of Lina, taken in Nice.

16. Jeanne Modigliani at an exhibition of her own paintings.

17. Jeanne Modligliani with her two daughters Anne and Laure.

expensive, if the countryside is truly interesting. It would be so kind if you could write to my brother.'

Later she wrote: 'My brother appeared to me yesterday morning just when I half-opened my eyes, which were still marked with night-time images from my dreams. I see – literally double.' André was away at the war. Germaine said that Max Jacob said Jeanne Hébuterne was psychic. She didn't use her powers, but she 'felt' people deeply and could tell their intentions without a word being said.

She constantly chided Germaine for being late: 'Don't be late. I wait to see you out of breath some thirty-five minutes late.' Her friend's lateness must have stood her in good stead for what came later. Did Modigliani arrive on the same day, let alone hour? Yet models and artists were surprised at his punctuality. He could be drunk the night before and make a date that they would assume he'd forgotten. But there he would be at the appointed time, early the next morning, shaved, bright-eyed, wearing clean clothes, ready to paint. Jeanne, so aware of time, saw that he kept appointments. She was good at taking care of people's lives. Encouraging Germaine to go for her job with the designer, she was precise in how to do it. She was good with financial arrangements – not so much for herself but for careless, carefree people like Modigliani, who threw his money around without a second thought.

Dear Bibi,

I am going to talk business. I've just seen the decorator a moment ago. He wants to see you here 6.30 to 7 on Thursday night. Have dinner with him and talk to him – warm him up a bit and speak in a precise way. Be clear about it. I am sure between here and Monte Carlo you could earn some money . . . You can set it up pretty fast. Anyway, my advice to you is set it up with him right away. Think of your freedom.

Above all, don't fail to show up.

She no doubt would have written such a letter to 'Dedo': 'Above all, don't fail to show up.' He didn't fail her – he came back. It wasn't

Jeanne's fault her mother had come. Or his. Zbo had involved her and let her come. Maybe it was for the best. It gave him freedom to work. He brought flowers for Jeanne, as he did for all the women he liked. Then he went to see Jacobelli's wife. Again.

Chapter Ten

However ill or depleted he was, Modigliani liked to feel clean. Max Jacob said that no matter how down the artist was, he always managed to be shaved, well groomed, with noticeably clean clothes. Whatever he put on he wore with style and distinction. Lunia said he always washed from head to foot in a tin basin after painting. By summer 1917 his teeth were beginning to go, and by the time of his death he had two plates of false ones. Chana Orloff said his breath smelt of drink; others remembered ether. He had few possessions but always carried his favourite books and a portrait of his mother. When he walked in the street his pockets were stuffed with pages of Leautréamont's *Les Chants de Maldoror*, which he believed influenced him more than anything else. He had a sturdy build and an obviously robust system to survive the excesses he put it through, even for such a short life.

He liked to walk and spent a great deal of time out of doors, which in itself improved his health. Sometimes he thought just by walking in the streets he could avoid death. He ran upstairs when he wasn't too drunk or hung over. A lot of energy and fire passed through that sick-robust body.

He had a security that he rarely mentioned. He himself may have forgotten it but in his worst moments, whirling downwards to nothing, he would be caught in time. His brother Emanuele, the Italian Socialist Deputy, would always come to his rescue, and he knew that there was a home waiting and a mother in it who would look after him. Jeanne had none of these things. How different her situation was to his! She had no one to break her fall.

So many people admired his way of working – it was absolute, assured. He was uncovering what was already there, enormous energy producing the finest, most delicate line. It went wrong only if he had to continue a picture for too many sittings. What he put on the canvas had to be done during the 'flare', the first energy. He'd prefer to start again than go back to an incomplete picture which had now 'died'. The model was posed, quite casually, then he concentrated on the expression, the feeling he saw in the face, not on its shape and colour or the features as such. Then he began sketching, paying no attention to the model, more concerned with conveying the essence of what he'd discovered. Then he laid on the paint, and in the finished composition he'd caught the truth of the person: manner, defence, sensuality, greed. Here was this person, even if they didn't like it. He wanted simplicity and clarity, not flattery. His sketching was so sure and fine that in one unbroken, enviable line he could swiftly convey a state of being. He was legendary in Montparnasse.

Foujita said he was also curious about other people's work: 'Once at Cagnes I was drawing a landscape. Modigliani came up behind me and watched for an hour. Then he tapped my shoulder and said, "Now I understand." He loved oriental things. He had a stylised art.'

But nothing was selling. Zborowski refused to give in. Foujita said that Zbo's method 'was to sit reading a paper in the esplanades or to go to the hotels, presumably with a rendez-vous with a duke or some important person, but nothing came of all this.'

It was time to move from Le Pavillon les Trois Sœurs and the other villas Zbo couldn't pay for.

Jeanne mentions two happy occasions during that time. One was their visit to the nearby village of Saint-Paul-de-Vence. Modigliani was excited by the church, its antiquity. The *curé* remembered how fast-moving and educated he was, how he ran all over the place and spoke Latin. And Jeanne, on the second occasion, remembered that the slow coastal train was full of light and colour and the sea outside the window was bright, but not as bright as the atmosphere in the carriage with its brown wooden seats and advertisements on the wall. She remembered that as a happy day. Her mother, in a letter to André, was surprised to find there were lovely moments in spite of the torturous worry.

Like her lover, Jeanne walked and sketched. She helped her mother prepare food. The grocer was at the top of the hill, the villa halfway down. The shops at the bottom, towards the sea, were cheaper. The way back up was unbelievably steep, almost to the point that 'it made you laugh'. It was now high summer.

Then came the night of the long knives. Modigliani arrived for dinner slightly drunk. Madame Hébuterne was contemptuous, so he reminded her of his origins. His family, the Modiglianis, were at one time bankers to the Pope in Rome. On his mother's side, scholars, philosophers, Spinoza – not the great Spinoza but if she chose to think it was, he would not dissuade her.

None of this made him good enough for her daughter, but he'd have to marry her. He became more outrageous, and when he was drunk he could brag. His niece, Madame Schalit, said he did not have a conventional background. On his mother's side they were all academic, full of ideas and poetry and freethinking, and she was proud of it.

The final row was described in *Artists' Quarter*: 'Madame Hébuterne, the mother-in-law to be ... particularly restive and angry, swore she would never have anything to do with him again and, cursing art and everything having to do with it for having robbed her of both her children, rushed to her room.'

These fights were about more than a marriage – they were a battle for Jeanne's soul. Her mother offered God's will, divine law and the path humans should tread so that they had a front seat on the Day of Judgement. Why be left out of glory? It was necessary to respect the Commandments.

Modigliani offered self-responsibility, not shoving it on to some deity's shoulders. He offered the chance to be truly alive – to be yourself, not the result of your parents and their thinking. Creation sometimes came out of tumult. Never out of the bourgeoisie!

Jeanne had to choose. She chose to have her baby. She didn't really have much choice, but she wanted to be well prepared to give birth.

For an instant Modigliani thought longingly of Livorno, just down the coast. He could make a run for it. But a war was on. He couldn't even cross the frontier. Instead, he moved in with Soutine.

In flight from the noise of the old man's trumpet, Soutine had moved in with the Jacobellis. They gave him a room in their crowded house, opposite Le Pavillon des Trois Sœurs. It still stands, but is now renovated and owned by the daughter of the mayor of Cagnes. Fernande Barrey and Foujita had moved in with the Zborowskis.

Fernande recalled how Soutine had not been seen for two days. She found him unable to leave his room until Zbo had sold a painting. He needed the money so he could eat. He had eaten nothing for two days. She took him back with her and gave him two slices of *gigot* – no more, otherwise there would have been nothing left for the others. The next day, a grateful Soutine brought Fernande a painting and an owl he'd found. He told her to choose which she wanted. Fernande chose the owl. No sooner had she taken it than it flew away. How Soutine laughed!

The Jacobellis, seeing that Soutine was starving even by their standards, gave him soup. Madame Jacobelli, still alive in 1989, is the niece of the farmer Jacobelli and his wife, Modigliani's model. She could remember her mother taking Soutine in and feeding him. He ate like one who had been starved for years. The countryside of Cagnes pleased Soutine and the Jacobellis, not understanding art as such but understanding pleasure, helped him to stay on when the others left.

Emile Lejeune remembered Modigliani moving in with Soutine. When the farmer's wife wasn't cleaning the village she was cooking and looking after her six children, all under nine. The two artists painted seriously for several days, then Modigliani got Soutine out on a drinking bout, which in retrospect Soutine hated. He never got over Modigliani or his death or his own anger at being persuaded to drink. However, those who knew him in Montparnasse said it didn't take the Italian to make him drink. As soon as he had one sou, Soutine was off to a bar.

Modigliani, needing more drink, took a painting to the grocer's shop at the top of the hill in Haut-de-Cagnes. Now that they knew him – although they were not famous for generosity – they allowed him drink in exchange for the painting. They didn't know what to do with it, so they displayed it on a shelf. Angelina said Modigliani returned for more credit the next day, and seeing the painting he broke into a rage. He took it off the shelf and destroyed it. It wasn't good enough. No amount of drink blanked out his sense of perfection. Wherever he lived – in Nice or Cagnes-sur-Mer – he always returned to paint Jacobelli's wife, to get credit from the grocer and drink in Rose's bar.

From the terrace of her rented villa Madame Hébuterne could see, through the trees, the Italian farmer's house, the Italian wife busy at her domestic tasks and the children playing in the sun. Then Modigliani appeared in the doorway and a certain languor, an excitement, would come over the Italian woman; her matter-of-fact actions with life's little chores slowed. Wiping back her hair, smoothing her dress, she'd go barefoot into the dark of the house. She was a different woman. Jacobelli's wife, the Italian girl; Modigliani's mistress – quite another matter. He brought out a woman's sexuality and mystery on canvas or on the bed.

And Madame Hébuterne slipped up to the grocer's and heard the scandal. She hurried to Jeanne. Tight-lipped, she told her the shattering news: Madame Jacobelli was pregnant. It would have any normal woman packing her bags, but how often Jeanne had heard that Modigliani slept with his models! It seemed essential for him to have some kind of sexual arousal with them while he painted them. They didn't get that look in their eyes from nothing. Jeanne wasn't a fool. She might be in love, but if he needed other women, she let him. It didn't mean she was generous or liked it, but she understood him. She felt there was nothing more to be said. He was what she wanted, and that need for the models was part of him. She could not change him. She knew he needed the balance within the imbalance to paint as he did. She could not deprive him of the drink or the hash pellets either. He was one of the last suffering artists, painters *maudits*. Very few people understood why she acquiesced. They thought it was because she was a victim – but in fact it was because she was strong.

95

Chapter Eleven

It was time for Zborowski to organise his flight to Nice. He put Modigliani in the Hôtel Tarelli, 4 rue de France; Jeanne and her mother in the rue Masséna, and Hanka and himself nearby. Foujita and Fernande Barrey took the train for Paris. Soutine stayed in Cagnes, or came back soon after. Foujita saw there was money either for train tickets or for rent. They chose the tickets. In retaliation Curel grabbed the good luggage, Foujita's and Zborowski's, but ignored the paintings. Foujita recalled how Père Curel died 'strangled with regrets'.

Emile Lejeune says the hotel where Modigliani stayed was frequented by prostitutes. He used to paint them and when he was ill with terrible flu they looked after him. Lejeune insisted that it was not the usual fantastic story one heard about the artist. He may or may not have slept with the girls, but they liked him enough to look after him.

Modigliani had old friends in Nice: Blaise Cendrars the writer and Swiss intellectual vagabond, Léopold Survage the Cubist artist and Gaston Modot, star and stuntman of silent films, with whom Modigliani had once shared a shack in the Maquis, at the top of Montmartre. He also visited the Russian sculptor Alexander Archipenko and behaved like a henpecked husband – the hen, presumably, being Madame Hébuterne.

The attack of flu shook him so badly that as soon as he could stand he gave up cigarettes and drink. He walked like an old man and sat at the farthest end of the Promenade des Anglais, away from the crowds and noise. Jeanne saw him in sharp contrast to the rest. Everyone wore light seaside clothes, while he wore black. Nice was a false playground, with everyone trying to have a good time and forget the war. It was a mixture of the rich, the fashionable, film stars and soldiers on leave. Jeanne couldn't compete with the fashions, but she had her own style, with her plaits wound round her head and long hand-made maternity dresses, some oriental in design.

Blaise Cendrars, who was writing a film script to be shot at the end of 1918, introduced her to some American friends, who gave her a maternity dress. Cendrars said she carried her baby 'in the teeth' – the French expression for high. Cendrars also gave a 1,000 franc note to his night *concierge* to give Modigliani if he should show up. Cendrars thought giving up drink was having a deleterious effect on his friend's humour. Every night when Cendrars returned to his hotel, the note was still there. Then, one day, it was gone: 'Cendrars thought *good* and he went through every bistro in Nice looking for Modigliani. He did not find him until he was coming in at six in the morning when he saw a man lying asleep in the middle of the place Iéna. It was, of course, Modigliani. From then on Modigliani lived as he had in Paris, and he got better.'

Modigliani sketched as he had in Paris, in the bars and cafés. Survage said he'd take his models from the street. It was time for Zborowski to go back to Paris but Lunia, taking over for him in the rue Joseph Bara, hadn't been able to sell any pictures. They were stuck. It was a grim thought.

Madame Hébuterne had written asking for money to be sent to her. André and Achille had both written to Jeanne. The baby must go to nuns for adoption and she must begin a new life. Madame Hébuterne was more worried than before. Cendrars said, 'Modigliani was in a bad way. You saw it at a glance.' She saw it in half a glance. She wanted him in church. That child must be baptised before he died.

Instinctively he knew his time was, at best, limited. However sensibly she put the proposition, anything coming from her was simply unacceptable. From Jeanne, yes – but Jeanne hadn't asked. By now it was painfully clear to the girl that he did not want to marry her. At the mention of church his Jewish origins, the services of his youth, stirred fleetingly. He remembered the grandfather he loved. Jeanne was not Jewish.

For once the fight was three-sided and Jeanne told her mother to keep out of it. Hanka intervened, quietened Modigliani, tried to soothe Madame Hébuterne and feed everybody and keep away creditors. Zborowski thought it was time to take Modigliani on a visit to a peaceful house, away from temptation, drink and demanding women.

Anders Osterlind, a friend of Zborowski, had a house in Les Collettes, near Renoir. His wife Rachèle was pretty, sympathetic and, like Modigliani, tubercular. They had a young daughter and a soothing, peaceful house. Around women like Rachèle, Modigliani was at his most charming and polite.

Osterlind wrote about Modigliani's stay:

Happy to welcome him, I gave Modigliani the best room, all white and clean, where he never did sleep very much. Coughing and thirsty, he spent the nights drinking by the jug and spitting on my walls as high as he could, looking on afterwards at the course of his saliva. He painted some beautiful things in this room, a beautiful portrait of a woman; he did several drawings too.

Zborowski furnished colours and canvas, and the exact amount of necessary alcohol which was useful and indispensable to his mental state. He kept hoping that Modigliani would not go down the narrow street leading to the section where lay the bistros in which he admired the advertisement – *Pernod fils* – a bottle and two glasses on a black background – whose beauty he extolled.

'*Mon vieux*', said Modigliani. 'They never made anything more beautiful than that!'

Jeanne Modigliani, while researching material for her book, talked to Osterlind, who said her father had stayed several months. She describes Rachèle as 'slowly dying of intestinal tuberculosis, the result of Spanish influenza. Modigliani painted her one day, seated in a rocking chair, her chin resting softly on her right hand. The portrait was later stolen from Osterlind and came to light again, slightly repainted, only a short time ago.'

The Osterlinds could see that Modigliani was sick and troubled, and they tried to help him. They offered him tea, which he politely declined and drank instead 'at a bar at the top of the Chemin des Collettes'. From here he made the long trek to Haut-de-Cagnes, up the steep hill to Madame Jacobelli.

If Modigliani was troubled and restless, so was Jeanne. She spent the nights burnt-eyed and sleepless in the hot room with the street noises going on until daylight. Her mind was full of him. She could see him vividly, as though he was with her. The baby moved, and it gave her definite pleasure. She loved having his child inside her – it was as though she was carrying a part of him. The mistake had been to let her mother insist on conventional behaviour. She'd been misled into thinking a pregnancy was a burden, an illness. Modigliani would never do anything against his will. From now on she, Jeanne, would defy her mother and the Church and just show him her love and devotion, get him back. But in truth she knew he hadn't gone.

The humidity of the weather didn't suit her – or him. His energy was low, his lungs were worse. His sarcasm was at its most acute. His mocking laugh was like that of a bird, and the Riviera was that bird's territory. Jeanne heard the bird – it usually travelled alone. It had a mocking laugh, like his. And sometimes she thought he'd come to visit. She asked the bird's name: 'A pie'.

When Modigliani painted the famous portrait 'The Little Girl in Blue' he was certainly angry. He sent the girl out for a bottle of wine and she came back with lemonade. He was furious, but the painting shows none of that. She stands transfixed, held by his gaze. This painting is considered his most tender and popular study of a child.

Further away in Toulouse, the windows of an art gallery had been shattered by stones. Students were reacting to a Modigliani nude in the window. The pubic hair offended them. Madame Marcellin Castaing, who later owned an antique shop on the rue Jacob, was passing with her husband. They too had escaped Paris and the shells of Big Bertha. They were so interested by the nude that they went into the shop and, after a process of bargaining, bought it and a portrait of a serving girl for 500 francs. Monsieur Castaing's parents were no doubt of the same mind as the Hébuternes. When the pictures were delivered they refused to have them inside their house and insisted they be returned to the gallery. Madame Castaing, however, found that Modigliani's work had made an unforgettable impression, and when she got back to Paris she bought forty drawings at 10 francs each. After Modigliani's death, another nude she wanted cost 6,000 francs.

Jeanne missed Modigliani. She went to look for him in Cagnes-sur-Mer. They told her he was up the hill near the château. It was twilight when she passed the villa she'd recently occupied. She continued towards the grocer's. She stopped to admire the air and view, which suddenly seemed magical. Then he appeared, part of the evening, its magic. He was pleased, surprised to see her. His eyes lit up. He held her arm, and sweetly asked what she was doing there. She said she wanted to see him. His face distorted with pain and he said, 'Go back to your mama.' Although he'd been in Rose's bar he did not seem drunk, but she felt he did not want her there, that she did not belong. Behind him appeared a good-looking Italian woman. Jeanne thought she remembered her from the village. Seeing Jeanne, she paused. This Italian woman had maturity and an obvious sexuality, pride and also the *savoir-faire* to please men. Jeanne took in all this at a glance. Modigliani spoke to her in Italian, then escorted Jeanne down the hill to the tram.

According to Jeanne Modigliani, her father never told the Osterlinds about Jeanne, her mother or the baby. They were quite astounded to learn that this 'family' had lived less than a mile away. He was either being discreet, or avoiding becoming part of that family.

Zborowski thought about Renoir. Ever hopeful, he said this was the way out: he'd arrange an introduction between his unacknowledged genius and the established one. Osterlind was the contact. Renoir, near death, crippled with arthritis, lived in semi-isolation. He was old and weak. Modigliani was drunk and nervous. This was the creator of the masterpieces that had heightened his life when he'd arrived in Paris. Here was the one man who understood women. No one could paint them like Renoir.

The visit was disastrous and has been described endlessly. Osterlind, who was apparently there, wrote an account:

Renoir's property was two hundred metres from my house, overrun by olive trees and rose bushes. This dwelling haunted Modigliani's imaginative spirit. He wanted to meet the master of Cagnes.

Returning one day from the village where he had at great length admired his favourite poster of *Pernod fils*, he said to me, 'Take me to Renoir.'

That very evening Renoir received us in his dining-room where he was brought after his work. It was a big bourgeois room. On the walls were some of his canvases. Also a delicate grey landscape of Corot which he liked.

The master lay crumpled in an armchair, shrivelled up, a little shawl over his shoulders, wearing a cap, his whole face covered with a mosquito net, two piercing eyes behind the veil.

It was a delicate thing putting these two face to face: Renoir with his past, the other with his youth and confidence, on the one side joy, light, pleasure and a work without peer, on the other Modigliani and all his suffering.

After Renoir had had some of his canvases taken down from the wall, a grim sombre Modigliani listened to him speak.

'So you're a painter too then, eh young man?' he said to Modigliani, who was looking at the paintings.

'__'

'Paint with joy, with the same joy with which you make love.'

'__'

'Do you caress your canvases a long time?'

'__'

'I stroke the buttocks for days and days before finishing a painting.'

It seemed to me that Modigliani was suffering and that a catastrophe was imminent. It happened. Modigliani got up brusquely and, his hand on the doorknob, said brutally, 'I don't like buttocks, monsieur!'

Renoir was seventy-seven and in acute pain. He had turned to sculpture, but the work had to be done by assistants. Since his wife's death he had been looked after by his housekeeper and maid. The house was run down, dying. Modigliani was deeply upset by the visit. Was it the sight of the old man in a decrepit state? The thought of him stroking buttocks? The contrast between what he had become and the glory of the early nudes? Renoir had always been a happy, sunny person. And now?

Jeanne, hearing that the visit had been unsuccessful, wanted to know why, but she was given no more satisfaction than anyone else. Modigliani was sarcastic or didn't respond. She, like the others, could only speculate. Renoir was the master, Modigliani anonymous. How the visit must have emphasised his failure! Maybe Osterlind had done too much kowtowing and obsequious talk before Modigliani even entered the room. How he hated that!

Zborowski wasn't beaten. A few weeks later he sent a letter; it happened that Renoir had seen an article Zborowski had written in a Paris magazine, praising him. Something of its style pleased the old master and he agreed to see him. He was impressed by Zborowski's dedication to bringing unknown artists into the light. He allowed him to sell two of his canvases. The commission gained would mean – freedom.

Zborowski sped to Marseille, taking the Renoirs and several Modiglianis. Kisling was on leave from the Front and saw him 'rushing about trying to interest dealers . . . most laughed at him for his pains'. Then Zbo got Jacques Netter interested and he bought ten Modiglianis for 500 francs, including 'The Little Girl in Blue', which years later, according to Hanka, Zbo was offered at 400,000 francs.

Now there was enough money to keep Modigliani painting and get Zborowski back to Paris:

It may be assumed that from that moment onward Modigliani never knew again the terrible destitution of his vagabond days, though he was not destined to enjoy his comparative prosperity for long. But as the months went by and fairly good news was coming from Paris he was no doubt cheered by the hope that the success for which he had struggled and suffered was now really within sight.

Chapter Twelve

Once the funds were forthcoming Modigliani sped back to Nice, and with his friend Léopold Survage drank in all the bars along the avenue de la Gare. Survage said that when he was drunk a madness seized him. He'd spend money on the soldiers on leave, a whole café full. He was doing just that on the evening his wallet, with all his papers, was stolen. Later Survage said it was his wallet, not Modigliani's. But in such a frenzy of drink one wallet could seem like a hundred. No papers, no wedding ceremony. Madame Hébuterne could see that.

Whatever mood he was in, he went back to Jeanne. Sometimes they'd take a walk by the sea or through the back streets. At others, Madame Hébuterne would tell him to get out and leave Jeanne in peace. The baby was due in November. She must not be worried. Madame Hébuterne wanted to hear only one thing: 'I will'. Modigliani was tender with Jeanne and promised they'd be together and he would be there when the baby was born, but he could not marry her – not without presenting her to his mother. This he would do when the time was right. Jeanne said she didn't want marriage either, but she didn't want to be denied the ultimate sanction of their love.

At this time Modigliani was running from hotel to hotel, never staying more than a few days before his riotous returns offended some hotelier. How he missed Jeanne! And she could not bear to be apart from him. But there were practical concerns: the baby, looking after it. Where would they live? Would he be there? No matter where they were, people always took him away, invited him for a drink, a meal, to be introduced to some painter. He was never hers. Sober, sincerely, he discussed the future. Things seemed to be looking up. If he did a series of paintings each month, then Zbo might give him an allowance against sales. They should live together. But Jeanne would have to be strong. Madame Hébuterne would have to go.

Again the Catholic woman went over all the arguments, adding that Modigliani wasn't giving her daughter the best, or what she deserved. He wasn't even giving her the best of himself. There was one final, terrible row. This time he did not argue. Jeanne did – she told her mother to go. After all she'd been through Madame Hébuterne nearly collapsed. Hanka helped her until she had recovered enough to move out. She took a room in another part of Nice. She would not leave for Paris until the baby was born – that was her duty. She saw her visit as a sacrifice. She also said, 'This child must not be born in sin.'

As far as Modigliani was concerned, sin belonged with the bourgeoisie.

Jeanne wanted to experience as much as she could, go as far as she could. That's what Modigliani had done, and she admired not so much what he'd done as his attitude to it. And there were the paintings – if he could do those, he must be blessed. Again she joined his unapplauded life.

Some of Survage's friends – like Germaine Meyer, whom he later married – never realised that Modigliani was ill. Meyer found him cultured in the French way, whereas Roch Grey, known as Baroness Oettingen, described his crazy piercing laughter as a spasm caused by a stomach convulsed with cold and hunger. He was 'vicious with vice. At his first view, even a partial one, of a well-formed female, he trembled with ardour, proving that love was the only real support on which his senses were ever entirely fixed.' Obviously she didn't like him. Perhaps, seeing her, he remained untrembling.

Armistice Day, 11 November 1918, was a night of wild celebration in Nice and Modigliani, with his friend Survage, gave it everything he had. The general optimism about the future also applied to him. His life could only get better.

Two weeks later his daughter Jeanne was born in Saint-Roch Hospital. He was enchanted. Out of all the bad times something good had come. He went to register the birth at the town hall but never got there: 'Unfortunately his celebrations of the happy event were so protracted that he finished by arriving there too late to do so. Afterwards he forgot this trivial matter, a fact which later was destined to cause tiresome complications.'

The complications arose when his brother Emanuele had to get the birth certificate to arrange the child's adoption. Emile Lejeune, in Haut-de-Cagnes at the time, said that Modigliani did not register the birth because the child was illegitimate – a thing to be kept quiet in those days. It is not even certain that the midwife entered the birth in the records. Lejeune said that the child was registered in her mother's name, Jeanne Hébuterne. Perhaps, he suggested, this is how she acquired the name Jeanne.

Madame Hébuterne stayed with her daughter until she had enough strength to look after the baby. It was clear that Modigliani was not going to marry her daughter, had never intended to, and Madame Hébuterne could do nothing but get on the train and leave. Somehow she must start her life again. She'd fought a good fight and lost. When Jeanne had first left home, Madame Hébuterne had used reason, then religion, then separation to bring her to her senses. Again she tried, but there was no force on earth that could keep Jeanne from Modigliani. Nevertheless, his work came first.

According to Lunia's statements, the birth and attending circumstances had been difficult and Jeanne 'kept bad memories of that time'. She was weak and suffering from postnatal depression. She wasn't in good enough shape to look after the baby properly. The endless nights of crying were draining her. There wasn't enough milk. She felt too ill and strange anyway – and then there was her mother's pain. What Jeanne felt for Modigliani did not minimise what she felt for others, but her mother didn't see it so simply. Before she left she promised the girl a bad end. He would provide that.

In the meantime Modigliani was scouring Nice for the right wet nurse. Cendrars's first wife Félicie wrote to Eugenia, Modigliani's mother, after his death:

> . . . Jeanne wore her plaits around her head like a coronet. I saw her for the last time around Christmas, after the birth of the child. We were all going to look for a wet nurse because neither she nor her mother could manage the child. Modigliani offered me a tangerine and also one to his wife (we were in front of a fruit store) – and that is my last memory of them.

Modigliani was very concerned about finding the right wet nurse. Survage said how it preoccupied him. He found a Calabrian girl in

Nice. He also wrote to his mother telling her she had a grandchild. It was her only one, apart from Gérard, the disputed son of Simone Thiroux. At some point her son Umberto, with whom Modigliani was not in touch, had a daughter. The Modigliani line ceased in that generation because there were no male children.

He spent New Year's Eve with Survage at the Coq d'Or restaurant. He sent Zbo a postcard 'on the stroke of midnight':

My Dear Friend,

I embrace you as I would have liked to do on the day you left us. I'm having a high old time with Survage here at the Coq d'Or. I've sold all my pictures.

Send me some money right away. The champagne is flowing like water. We send you and your dear wife best wishes for the New Year.

Resurrecto Vitae.

Hic incipit vita nova.

Il novo Anno!

The champagne was flowing, so was the optimism – Modigliani hadn't sold anything, and he was broke. Jeanne stayed at home and looked after the baby.

Chapter Thirteen

Survage had a two-room flat in Nice. He lived in one room and in the second Modigliani painted. Survage remembers a portrait of a soldier, but often the models did not show up. Survage thought that people in Nice were not particularly fond of posing. He sat for Modigliani and found it a curious picture because one eye was uniformly coloured, iris and white all the same, with no pupil; and the other was normal. Survage asked why and Modigliani said, 'With one eye you look outward, with the other you look inside.'

Modigliani painted Jeanne at their home at 13 rue de France. As he mentioned in a letter to Zborowski, 'I am waiting till a little head of my wife is dry before sending you, along with those you know about, four canvases.' He also did a portrait of his daughter in the arms of the nurse, on which he spent a great deal more time than usual. Modigliani had agreed a deal with Zborowski: each month he'd receive an allowance from Paris in exchange for several paintings. The arrangement ran into snags. First there was the lost wallet, in which he said he had had 600 francs. (Survage thought that was a huge amount for Modigliani to have at any one time.) So he needed extra money to keep him going, and more to repay Survage a 100 franc loan. Money was also required for Jeanne and the nurse. According to Survage, when the allowance did arrive Modigliani would go straight to the bars in the avenue de la Gare and celebrate. Survage thought Jeanne got her hands on very little. The other recurring problem was the business of the lost papers. Without them he couldn't leave Nice.

He wrote to Zbo: 'Apart from the money lost, the question of the papers is an even greater worry. That was about all I needed, just when I had a little peace.'

Later, in a letter dated 27 February 1919, he wrote: 'Thanks to my brother, all that to-do over my papers has been taken care of. As things stand now I can leave when I please. I am still tempted to stay on, going back early in July.'

It seems that at last Modigliani was happy. He wrote to his mother: 'Dearest Mother, I am here right near Nice. Very happy . . .' He'd told her about the baby and she'd already replied warmly. In his next letter he says:

Dearest Mother,
A thousand thanks for your affectionate letter. The baby is fine and so am I. It doesn't astonish me that having been so much a mother you now feel like a grandmother even without 'legal sanction'.
I am sending you a photograph.
I have a new address: write 13 rue de France, Nice.
I kiss you warmly.
Dedo.

He doesn't mention Jeanne, or getting married, but the letters describing her may well have been destroyed after her tragedy. He was very compartmentalised in his relationships. To his mother he spoke reassuringly. He doesn't mention Zbo either.

The baby was in blooming health. How relieved they both were! No sign of tuberculosis. And Modigliani, with occasional lapses, worked continuously. The change of season affected him. He wrote to Zbo:

The way things are going, the changes of pace, especially the change of season, makes me fear a change in the weather and my rhythm . . . Let's give things a chance to grow and develop. I've been taking it easy. The last few days, fruitful laziness. That's real work.
And now for the Survage story in two words. Little pig. But enough of that. Are you coming down in April . . .

'Little pig' has caused much speculation. Survage said it referred to an occasion when they were both courting the same woman. Survage won. Jeanne Modigliani said it was apparently Lunia.

What could Jeanne do? She knew, had always known, that there was a certain heightened tension between Modigliani and the Polish woman. Questions wouldn't get her anywhere. Every day he went off to paint, and every evening he went out to drink. Survage said he saw Jeanne rarely. He remembers the three of them taking coffee, and then Modigliani putting her on the tramway so she could go back to her mother, whom he never saw at all. Survage said Jeanne was a very gentle, kind person who drew tiny still lifes on sheets of letter-sized paper. She gave one to Survage; much later he gave it to her daughter. Survage believed that his friend lived only for his painting and had no other attachment. He said 'even the Hébuterne episode was secondary', although the child was very important.

Modigliani put a different face on for his male friends. He didn't want to appear tied down or bourgeois, or in the hands of a woman. He kept Jeanne very much to himself; it was a private business. Jeanne Modigliani's explanation for her father's behaviour is that he did things in the Italian way: he kept his wife at home as a sign of respect. She would never be allowed in a bar.

Jeanne made clothes for herself and the baby, sketched, took walks, made meals. Under everything was a lurking depression. She still wasn't well. He was very kind and solicitous. He was absolutely enchanted by and absorbed in the child she'd borne him, and he knew the sacrifices she'd made to be with him. While he was receiving loving letters from his mother and supportive ones from Zbo, she got two from her father and brother which she kept to herself.

Then came Zbo's big news: there was to be a London show. Sacheverell Sitwell had come to Paris wanting to sponsor, with his brother Osbert, an exhibition of modern French art in London that summer. As Zbo represented Modigliani he was invited to help choose and supervise the shipping of the canvases, then come to London himself and assist in the selling. Sitwell didn't have sufficient funds to buy a Modigliani painting, but he did buy a drawing. In his book *Laughter in the Next Room* Sir Osbert Sitwell says that Sacheverell joined him in Biarritz and brought 'a very fine Modigliani drawing'.

This was what Zbo had been on his knees for. He was emotional with happiness. Modigliani would now be recognised far beyond Paris. All the years of hard work and suffering, defeats and ill luck – surely worth it.

Modigliani wrote back with his biographical details necessary for the catalogue and newspaper publicity. He said he was sincerely moved:

> Another thing . . . you speak of coming here toward the end of April. I think I can easily wait for you here until then. Meantime as I go right ahead you should look at the possibility of settling in Paris as there is a great 'hic' [difficulty]. Are you ever going to look into the Montmartre business? My daughter is getting astonishingly bigger. I find great comfort in her and I think that can only increase in the future . . .

The 'Montmartre business', already mentioned, was the rue Ravignon affair, referred to twice in his correspondence with Zborowski. The exact details have never been clarified. He did live there. He did know Elvira, one of his nude models, there. As for the 'difficulty', that was never understood either. It could well have been Jacobelli's wife, who had given birth to his daughter Lina. The 'settling in Paris' would refer to himself, not Zbo.

Jeanne saw that he was hopeful, more so than he'd been since he'd left Paris. She saw too that his life in some measure demanded hers. She had to be there for him. He gave her no choice – he demanded everything . . . all. Life in the rue de France was domestic because it contained the baby. It was optimistic and light, with open windows letting in sea air. This was their happiest and sweetest time, full of laughter. Jeanne wrote that for a short time everything seemed light and effortless and the scorched feeling of pain and rejection was quite gone. Because he was happy, she was.

And then, quite suddenly, he'd had enough of Nice. He was now joining Zbo and the excitement of the London show. He wanted to get back into the mainstream. Maybe now he would have that piece of success to show his mother.

Jeanne did not want him to go. She wanted the good, sweet time to go on, never end. She sensed that if he left, it would be broken and never recaptured. She fought to keep him with her and little Jeanne in Nice. She lost. Carrying a safe-conduct pass issued by the Cagnes police, he left by train on 31 May 1919. He promised Jeanne he would be gone only a few days. He'd arrange a place and a nurse for the baby. He'd come back and get her. Of course, Lunia was in Paris.

Chapter Fourteen

The second baby was never intended. She waited to tell him, but he didn't come back. The letters were frequent and reassuring and he sent money, so she went on expecting him. Also she needed him – obsessively, addictively. But she knew that being with someone all the time was not his way. He liked new people, variety. Sometimes he was bored by her, sometimes by himself. Fortunately, she was capable of being on her own.

He was in Paris with Lunia, painting her, going out with her in the evenings. Lunia said that he liked being looked after and always ended by doing everything she asked him, even to the extent of giving up drinking. She talked him into taking his health and addictions seriously. She wanted him to get well and live for his daughter's sake. Her memories of that time are sweet, she says. While she posed he talked his heart out to her. He talked about his mother, Livorno, the child – the dearest things. No mention of Jeanne Hébuterne – not in Lunia's recollections. He told her he wanted to live near his mother in Italy and regain his health. To be completely happy he needed only to have his daughter, a house with conventional furnishings. He wanted a dining-room. He wanted, she said, to live like everyone else: 'With his Latin exuberance these were dreams without end.' Sichel, in his biography, remarks: 'They were also dreams without Jeanne apparently, and the omission is possibly Lunia Czechowska's. But the absence of Jeanne Hébuterne in this idyll is as conspicuously uncharacteristic as is his odd desire to live in bourgeois conformity *à la* Matisse.'

After he'd painted Lunia, they would go and sit on the terrace of the Rotonde or the Closerie des Lilas and then to Rosalie's for supper. Rosalie adored Modigliani; he was her god. She made him special dishes spiced with garlic. They were so good that he told Lunia: 'When I eat garlic it's as if I kissed the mouth of the woman I love.' Rosalie was always trying to stop him drinking, saying he was a disgrace to Italy.

In *Amedeo Modigliani*, Lunia wrote:

After dinner we used to walk in the Luxembourg Gardens. It was very hot that summer. Sometimes we went to the cinema, other nights we strolled around Paris. One day he took me to a street fair to show me La Goulue, Toulouse-Lautrec's favourite model, who appeared in a cage with some wild animals. It reminded him of other times and he recalled that era at length, the painters and figures who have since become famous. We walked and walked, often stopping by the little wall along the Luxembourg Gardens. He had so many things to talk about that we were never able to say good night. He spoke of Italy, which he was never to see again, and of the baby he was never to see grow up, and he never breathed a word about art the whole time.

She said how fastidious he was. One particular afternoon in this summer, 'heavy with heat and annoyances', he wanted to wash and placed the basin on the window ledge of Zbo's flat. It toppled and crashed down into the street. The terrible *concierge*, *La Mère* Salomon, looked up and screamed curses at him. How she hated the tramps – him, Utrillo and Soutine! Finally, to annoy her more, he perched on the window ledge naked and sang. Lunia was scared he would fall and invited him into the Zborowskis' flat for dinner. She said he always enjoyed eating there with her and, still singing, he got dressed and calmed down. While she was preparing supper he asked her to look at him, and by the light of a candle he drew a beautiful sketch. On it he wrote: '*La Vita e un Dono: dei pochi ai molti: di Coloro che Sanno e che hanno a Coloro che non Sanno e che no hanno.*' [Life is a Gift: from the few to the many; from Those who Know and have to Those who do not Know and have not.]

Modigliani had a direct relationship with his models, not letting any outside influence intervene. No abstract or intellectual considerations were allowed near him. He told Survage he needed a living model in front of him in order to paint. Abstraction was a dead end: 'Beware of falling to the depths of the unconscious. Chaos must be organised.'

Jeanne waited. The London exhibition would take him away. The London art scene would want him next. Again he would not be entirely hers. Towards the end of June she panicked. She knew –

how she sensed it! – that he was with Lunia. For the first time she seriously thought he might leave her, but he loved the baby. Finally she sent a telegram. She addressed it to the Zborowskis' flat in the rue Joseph Bara: 'June 24, 1919: Need money for trip. Wire 170 francs plus 30 for nurse. Letter follows. Arriving Saturday at 8 o'clock by express. Let nurse know.'

When she arrived in Paris there was no nurse, but Lunia and Hanka had redecorated and cleaned the studio in the rue de la Grande Chaumière in preparation for the baby. She finally got him alone and told him about the new baby. He said, quite steadily, 'We don't have luck.'

Five days before his thirty-fifth birthday he signed a document which he himself had written on a sheet of lined grey paper: 'I pledge myself today, July 7 1919, to marry Mademoiselle Jane Hebuterne as soon as the papers arrive.' It was signed by Amedeo Modigliani, Leopold Zborowski, Jeanne Hébuterne, and Lunia Czechowska. At the bottom right: 'Paris July 1919'. He left the acute accent off 'Hébuterne' and an 'e' and 'n' out of 'Jeanne'. Did he think that by making her English he could avoid the marriage? There was an afterthought about the date – adding the year in afterwards, trying to make it legal. The papers? Hadn't his brother sorted them out? How could Jeanne know whether the missing papers had arrived or not? She did not want to end up like Simone Thiroux. For a while she was as adamant with him as she had been with her parents.

Hanka's name is an omission which meant she wasn't present at the time. If her husband signed it she would have, in spite of her ambivalent feelings towards Jeanne.

Very shortly after writing and signing this pledge, Modigliani wrote to his mother. The letter is dated the same day. Perhaps he intended to tell her of his plan. Instead he said he was thinking of coming home. This letter was later given to his daughter:

Paris 7 Juillet 1919

Chère Maman,

I send you a photo. Je regrette de ne pas en avoir de ma Fille. Elle est à la campagne – en nourrice.

Je médite pour le printemps peut-être un voyage en Italie. Je voudrais y passer une période. Ce n'est pas sûr quand même ...

Dedo

113

It is clear, from the errors in the document and this letter to his mother, that he could not commit himself to another woman. His mother already had him, in so many ways. The ambivalence from which he suffered was now pierced. He went out and got drunk.

Jeanne used the document as a guarantee to convince her parents and God that she was now spiritually correct. Another child? Monsieur Hébuterne was beside himself. Most women had a function in life: to look after a husband, to work in a department store, to be a nun or even an artist, as she'd once wanted. But to keep bringing children into the world, children she couldn't look after and nobody wanted. What kind of career was that? Jeanne tried for a reconciliation, witnessed by her childhood friends, like Gabriel Fournier and Stanislav Fumet, but it had all gone too far.

The change of air, the dust in the studio, the absence of the Calabrian nurse, the lack of fresh sea smells, upset the baby. Jeanne was trying to prepare milk correctly for her bottle, while her 'husband' was occupied with other bottles. The baby cried incessantly. Jeanne was already feeling ill with the new pregnancy. There was no proper air unless she went to the Luxembourg Gardens but then a pram had to be arranged and carried to and fro, up the stairs. Modigliani finally snapped. He'd had it. He could no longer bear the noise of the unhappy baby, more responsibility to come. Who would pay for it? How did he know the London show would be any good? They'd said the same about the Berthe Weill exhibition, which had failed.

Jeanne shouted back. What had he done for a month in Paris? Except paint Lunia. Wouldn't she like to have the time to paint? It was all on her back. And where were the new flat and the new nurse? She couldn't take any more. It couldn't get worse. It could: Lunia arrived.

The shouting was not good for the baby. Jeanne was exhausted, overwrought. She never slept. The baby cried continually. Modigliani was out all night. She had morning sickness. She wasn't eating properly. Lunia was all concern for Jeanne. What she really meant was: you've put all this responsibility on him, and now he's ruined! Lunia said she would take the baby to the Zborowskis until Jeanne felt better. They'd try to get a nurse.

Modigliani, semi-drunk, did what he always did. He went to the Rotonde and this time he took his baby with him.

Gabriel Fournier was so surprised by the sight he came over and asked whose baby it was. Modigliani said his and Fournier congratulated him.

No nurse would stay in the studio. It didn't have facilities, wasn't right for a nurse or a baby. Modigliani was wildly drunk, his health cracking. Paris was a disappointment. He'd rushed back hopeful at last for some recognition. Neither the public nor the critics knew of him or cared. Paris might be changed after the war but it was no better for him. His contemporaries were all doing well. Less talented artists, even his friends, even Utrillo were doing better. Zborowski kept saying, the London show. Wait for that. But nothing ever came out of Zbo's hope. Even Jeanne knew that.

Jeanne got her baby back from Lunia. She tried again. He arrived, half falling up the stairs, and started shouting. The baby started crying. The depression, a knife in Jeanne's side, was not really lifting, even with drink. The baby went back to Lunia. It was obvious she wanted his baby. She loved him. Jeanne saw that.

The Zborowskis blamed Jeanne. Before she came back to Paris he was working and sober. Now he was a wreck. Unrecognisable. How could she impose a second baby on him? How could she when he was trying so hard and with such lamentable health? How could she ruin him? Zbo was almost crying, all the pent-up horror of Nice was bubbling out of him.

Jeanne felt too depressed to argue back. Of course they'd always been against her. They blamed her for the way in which her mother insulted and upset him. The way he had no peace to work.

She didn't retaliate because they were all he had when it came down to it. His hopes arose from them and died with them. They didn't go anywhere else, it seemed. And they were on his side. She would not cause a confrontation where he might have to choose. She put him first.

She went back to her studio still hearing the cries of the baby. All the peace of the Riviera quite gone. She knew if she was going to keep Modigliani, keep him on the earth, he had to win the battle against drink. He had to choose to remain here and for that he had to overcome bitterness, drugs, drink, wild living and a growing sense of suspicion that the world was against him. And yet this was the background, the chemical balance he now needed to work. It wasn't painting any more, then life, then some days of illness. Now it was painting, then illness. As usual, she decided to be there for him. The baby would have to be placed in a nursery for the time being. Then he came towards her across the noisy floorboards, pulled her to him. There was no longer any reason to take care.

Lunia described how Modigliani would show up with Utrillo, both drunk, wanting to see the baby. They'd call up at the Zborow-skis' flat. No reply. When he was drunk, he was not allowed near that baby:

> Both of them then sat on the footpath facing the building and Modigliani called up to me for news of the baby. He stayed there for hours and my heart was torn to see him so unhappy. We didn't turn on the lights so he would think we had all gone to bed. Then he'd go off sadly with his friend. If I'd been alone, I certainly would have let him come up. Sometimes they gave in to my pleas; then he'd come up and sit next to his child, looking at her with such intensity that he ended up falling asleep himself; and I watched over both of them. Poor dear friend, those were the only moments that he had his little daughter all to himself.

Lunia was a marvellous and lucky model for him. Perhaps it was the underlying intensity of feeling that made the paintings so exquisite. They have been described as striking, with a warm wistful loveliness, elegant, fine – and they sold. Jacques Netter bought two 'Lunias' at 150 francs each.

Finally they found the right nursery for the baby, in Chaville near Versailles. Jeanne Modigliani said the correspondence with the nurse 'represents an accurate idea of the Modigliani–Hébuterne ménage: telegrams, gifts and baby bonnets alternating with long silences.' Jeanne made regular visits. Every week she took the train to see her child. Modigliani went once. With the baby settled, he went back to painting and Lunia said it was the time of his best pictures. They were of herself, Hanka and Jeanne. He packed a lot into that summer. Time? He was not sure how long he had.

Chapter Fifteen

Zborowski went to London for the Sitwell-sponsored show in July. He sent a telegram to Hanka: 'Lunia sold for 1,000 francs bought by Arnold Bennett'. Bennett particularly liked Modigliani's portraits because they conjured up the heroines of his novels. The Sitwells bought 'Peasant Girl'. Modigliani and Utrillo were the sensations of the show.

Modigliani received the first good reviews of his life. A London Jewish newspaper was particularly praising, and he kept that in his pocket along with his treasured *Chants de Maldoror*. He asked Zbo to bring him back a pair of English shoes.

Francis Carco, one of his truest and staunchest admirers, who had bought the pink nude when he could ill afford it, praised his work in *L'Éventail*, a Swiss magazine. Modigliani sent the clippings and magazine straight to his mother. Carco's article appeared in July 1919. The August edition showed reproductions of the drawings. Modigliani was getting the notice he wanted in unexpected places – but not in Paris.

When Zbo returned there was a good celebratory feeling and the explosive scene with Jeanne was forgotten. The Russian painter Marevna Vorobev saw Modigliani in summer 1919. He said he was earning money, had two children and was becoming respectable. Next he'd be fat. Inside he was laughing. She took him seriously.

Umberto Brunelleschi, one of his early Italian friends, returned to Paris at the end of the war. He ran into Modigliani, 'ravaged and unkempt' – ironically, making a sketch of a beggar. As always Modigliani, seeing a friend, was warm and emotional. He opened his arms wide, clasped Brunelleschi. But he didn't show up at Rosalie's for dinner. He was already drunk somewhere else.

Another old friend, Anselmo Bucci, went to the studio in the Grande Chaumière looking for Modigliani. He found the building gloomy. He described Jeanne opening the door – 'a tiny transparent waif of a woman with a waxen-white face'.

'Modigliani is not home. I am Madame Modigliani.'

Bucci found his friend in the Rotonde: '. . . after such a long stormy time he was quite natural and almost wholesomely human as I hadn't seen him in fifteen years.'

They talked about the war, and Modigliani said, 'I wanted to go on foot all the way to the Front but when I reached the end of the boulevard I was dissuaded. What about you, though? Gone and been a hero for the Futurists?' The Futurists was a group Modigliani loathed and refused to belong to.

They went to eat at Rosalie's. Jeanne joined them. Bucci noticed that Modigliani, a typical alcoholic, ate little. He was 'most affectionate toward Jeanne, almost ostentatiously petting her, talking to her, asking questions'. Afterwards they went back to the Rotonde. On the way Modigliani told Jeanne to go home, '. . . hugging and kissing her with a great show of affection and waving at her from afar'. Modigliani said to Bucci, 'We're going to the café, just the two of us. My wife goes home in the Italian way. Are you surprised?'

Roger Wild and Germaine Labaye frequently ate with Jeanne and Modigliani in Les Trois Portes. Roger Wild said, 'He could be so articulate, polite and loving. In drink he was impossible. No one could handle him.' There is no doubt that Jeanne suffered.

The show in London had got good reviews and a few sales, but that didn't mean Paris had to know about it – or care. The city, like a hostile woman, turned on Modigliani, flung her furs around her and haughtily walked off, jewels jangling. She would never be his.

He saw it before they did. Salmon said that about this time he started to grimace and say continuously *Sans blague*. He likened this to the behaviour of Baudelaire near death, and said it had a long medical name.

Zbo was now able to give him a regular allowance, but it was never enough. Kisling said, 'If you have 2,000 francs a month and spend 1,900 on alcohol you must expect to live in misery. Modi never knew when to stop.'

The next step of hope for Zborowski was the Salon d'Automne from November to December the 12th at the Grand Palais. Modigliani was to show four paintings. He'd entered two of those exhibitions

– one in 1907, the next in 1912 – without success. Although Zbo had hope, Modigliani did not.

His paintings deepened, became testaments. Still an outcast, he would not be seduced by fame. In certain moods he saw that the lines had gone beyond technique and were the stark outline of the other territory, between reality and death; an uncomfortable place where hallucinations swirled like storms and three-dimensional safety was gone. He could pay the price, stay and see. Jeanne told him not to drink. She had to persuade him to eat. She didn't bother about the cigarettes. She said she was going to visit the baby. Did he want to come? Not this visit. He could get to the Rotonde. Just. After a few drinks he got as far as Montmartre and said his goodbye to Suzanne Valadon. His friend Utrillo, her son, was now institutionalised and the news saddened him. He sang songs, including the Kaddish, the Jewish lament for the dead. He went off into the dark – not laughing. Suzanne Valadon said he looked ill and worn out. Max Jacob saw it too. He tried to tell him to take care, knew it was pointless. He drew up the baby's horoscope. He greatly admired his friend for his understanding of great poetry. After his death he wrote, 'Your life of simple grandeur was lived by an aristocrat. We loved you.'

Ortiz saw it and tried to sneak him up food from his wife's meagre table. He thought Zborowski should do something about it, but the rumour was out: Zbo, like so many dealers, preferred the dying. A dead painter was a superb investment. When Ortiz could not get a dealer, Sandahl suggested Zborowski. 'Oh no,' said Ortiz, 'he won't take on my work. I'm not sick.'

In the end Lunia did something: she asked him to come away with her. She would take him to the Midi and he would recover. The Zborowskis were all for it. It was possibly his last chance. This was discussed at their flat in the rue Joseph Bara. Modigliani was thoughtful. They told him how good Lunia was for him – the implication being that Jeanne wasn't.

When he went home to Jeanne he was not only sober, but sombre, and she felt the first trickles of icy panic, like winter beginning. 'Nothing changed after the London show,' he said. 'It made no difference in Paris.' His work sold spasmodically. His was no success story. He had been hopeful for the last time. He had to ask himself if this was indeed Paris – or hell.

Jeanne could see pain, bitterness, and she prayed that just one thing could come right for him. One break. She saw how he was changed: reserved, inward-looking. She thought – he loves Lunia. It was true, and yet again it wasn't. It was the rejection of his work that silenced him.

Lunia waited for his answer. She was sure it would be yes.

The studio reflected the state of its occupants. It was run down and covered in coal dust, cigarette butts. One of his last models, Thora Klinckowstrom, offered to sweep it. She thought the dust was making his cough so bad. Quite brusquely he said he wanted it left alone. Thora was introduced to 'my wife', whom she remembered as a small reserved woman with plaits, obviously pregnant, who then withdrew to another part of the studio. He was still, in spite of his condition, very attractive – Thora found him so.

After the sitting he washed his face ready for the Rotonde. Jeanne clung to him, to keep him with her, not for his health but for herself. She couldn't bear the long lonely hours . . . the studio was now a prison. Those once peaceful, harmonious times of being alone had become intolerable. Her clinging brought out the worst in him. Over-possessiveness – how he hated that! In his view it had nothing to do with love: it was a prison: 'I don't want to see your face always in front of mine. Everywhere I look.' As though struck, she reacted with pain. He dragged up his coat, got cigarettes. Then he suddenly stopped and said something funny and she laughed. It was all right – for now.

The next time the studio was unbearable she wrote it all to Germaine, although Modigliani's drunken evenings had put paid to their close friendship. She'd had to take his side. He was more and more vitriolic. She agreed with his reason for being angry, but not with what he said – or to whom. But she couldn't say anything. He allowed her no space. His reaction to her offer of advice was immediate and so violent that she lapsed into silence. And around her he was often silent. There was a lot of silence in that studio. It felt as though they were waiting – supposedly for the baby. Then she looked out at the tree in the courtyard rather as a prison inmate might. But the door wasn't locked. She opened it and went down to the de Zárates. Then she remembered they wouldn't be pleased to see her and she was too dignified to ask for their help. She went back up to the studio with its noisy floorboards and waited for the uneasy mood to pass. Outside, people were having a good time. There were balls and parties and impromptu dancing at the Vavin crossroads. Modigliani could be at the little all-night café on the boulevard de Vaugirard near Marie Wassilieff's. The poker game was still going on in the Dôme. He wouldn't be there. In fact he was in a cemetery reciting Dante.

She had to go and look for him in the Rotonde because he didn't come back. That often meant he'd picked a fight and been arrested. This time his absence was legal: he'd been talking with Lunia. When he returned he said he was going to the Midi.

Immediately she said, 'With Lunia'. It was as though a knife had pierced her heart. Afterwards she made a drawing of it. It became the first of a series of ways she visualised dying.

He said, 'To work. What else?' But then he saw he couldn't leave her. Theirs had been a passion. Intense colliding contacts weren't meant to drag on and die in bourgeois style. They could be finished in a night. That's how it was in the Bohemian world. But friendship was something else. Eternal. He said she should come too.

The next day Lunia and the Zborowskis waited in the street. Modigliani came down coughing. Jeanne followed, tight-faced and exceptionally white. Lunia noticed that he wasn't carrying luggage – not a good sign. He said he would go, but Jeanne must come too. Jeanne said she had a child in a nursery and another due to be born in January. Her memories of the first birth weren't wonderful. She'd stay in Paris. She was booked into the Tarnier clinic, where all the artists had their children.

What she really meant was, 'No, Lunia. You can't have him.'

But he had choice. He could go. They weren't exactly married. He said he'd stay with Jeanne, and then the row really started. Lunia left very emotionally. Before she went she kissed 'Modi' and afterwards frequently sent him flowers. The Zborowskis looked at Jeanne as though she'd passed a death sentence. They never forgave her.

Lunia writes: 'I could do nothing for him since he had a wife. Zborowski saw things differently. My principles, not just bourgeois, but of simple moral honesty regarding another woman held me back. I knew that Jeanne Hébuterne loved him and for me that was sacred.' Zborowski had urged her to go to any lengths to force Modigliani to take care of his health. She was also implying that Jeanne wasn't doing enough.

Lunia continues, '. . . but since I couldn't be his, he [Modigliani] couldn't stand my belonging to another man.' Apparently he'd learnt that she was seeing someone else and criticised her so much that she began to feel upset: 'I was to remain the spiritual friend. Such was my destiny. I was young and probably romantic. I had to abstract my feelings since another person needed me. I had no experience of life and acted by pure intuition. I forced myself not to fall in love with the man I had met.'

She said her own bad health obliged her to go to the Midi to recuperate. Her friends insisted she take Modigliani, and he wanted to go: 'But Jeanne Hébuterne was expecting her second child and the idea of leaving Paris depressed her. She had sad memories of the time when Giovanna was born; and the idea of Modigliani going without her distressed her just as much.'

Some of their friends believed the 'rival' was a fiction to arouse Modigliani and get him to go with her – or a way of not losing face when he stayed with Jeanne. It was obviously a highly charged time for all of them, and after it his fate was sealed.

Chapter Sixteen

Modigliani's desire to paint was his own. It had nothing to do with the hostile outer world, people's judgement or preference, or even money any more. Jeanne heard the endless cough, saw the spitting of blood. His voice was nearly gone. His hair was flat, even his eyes were dull. He walked the streets hoping to recover, to lose death. He called it the man in the hallway who wished him no good. It had left the hallway and started to come up the stairs. He couldn't handle drink. Some days one glass would finish him. It was November and Jeanne tried to get him to see a doctor. She'd go with him. She pleaded with him. Then Zborowski came round and told her she must get a doctor. Couldn't she even see he was seriously ill? She invited Zborowski to try. She'd done her best.

Zbo suggested a clinic. Modigliani didn't quite laugh in his face. He knew he was done for. He did, however, buy some medicine.

Now it was December and he no longer took care of himself. He was dirty and had allowed a beard to grow. Everybody was against him. How he hated it all! She told him to go to Italy. She'd come with him. She tried to reason as her mother had with her – for the good of the thing. His only physician was death.

However ill he became, he would not go back to Italy without a gift for his mother; the gift of success. His father had failed. Did he have to fail as well? Sometimes his mother's continuing and insistent belief in him choked him. Out he went into the streets. Jeanne said she'd go with him and got her coat. These weren't lovers' walks he was on. He was a limping dog finding a place to die.

He walked in the early morning, a serious man with profound eyes, pale faced unshaven, knowing that death was already there, waiting. He considered an escape back to Italy, to prolong life a little in his mother's care. But all he wanted was to seize the next hours and paint, just until that picture was complete and he replete. And then, full of stimulants and drugs which had been necessary to allow him the respite to work, he would subside, sicker than before, into a misery only drink could shut out.

He wrote a poem:

> From upon the black mountain, the king,
> the chosen to rule, to command
> weeps the tears of a man who could not
> reach the stars,
> And from the dark crown of clouds
> fall drops, pearls, in the extravagant night heat.

Louis Latourettes, a financial journalist, saw him in Montparnasse and thought he looked 'pale, feverish and emaciated. He had been drinking heavily, a pile of saucers registering the numerous drinks he had already consumed.'

Modigliani said, 'Say hello to the cherry tree on top of the rue Lepic. Say that I could never get to eat its fruit. The kids of the rue Norvins always got there first, before the cherries ripened.'

Libion, former owner of the Rotonde, invited him for a drink and he admitted he was done for. Then he cheered up suddenly and talked of going back to Italy. 'He said his mother would get him well. She knew best.'

Amazingly, he rallied and went off early one morning to see his daughter in the nursery. He came back in good spirits and painted Jeanne against the door of the studio, then Paulette, the Zborowskis' maid. He had days, even now, when he was so sunny that Paulette could not believe how ill he was.

Ossip Zadkine described his last days among people: 'I think he saw through those who were taking care of him but he said nothing. And then he loved Mademoiselle Hébuterne . . . his friend who was then his only friend. A real person, for she was good and beautiful and had a beautiful soul.'

His sarcasm upset many people, but one still came to the door: Simone Thiroux, hearing that he was so ill, wanted to see him. Jeanne had no time to give sympathy and didn't let her in. Modigliani wasn't home. His health worse, he was at the Zborowskis' refusing a doctor. After all she'd been through, Jeanne realised he still did not belong

125

to her. He belonged to the Zbos, the streets, the cafés. He belonged to drink.

He still had energy to sleep with Jeanne, a voracious last grasp at life. And afterwards they lay shivering together. It felt as though they were in a raft, but sinking.

At Christmas his mother sent him a loving note:

I hope, my very dear Dedo, that this arrives just on the first morning of the year, as if it were a sweet kiss from your old mother, bringing with it every blessing and every possible good wish. If there is such a thing as telepathy you will feel me near you and yours.

A thousand kisses,
Maman

Simone Thiroux sent another:

Dearest Friend,
My tenderest thoughts turn to you on the occasion of this new year, which I so much hope will be one of moral reconciliation for us. I put aside all sentimentality and ask for only one thing, which you will not refuse me since you are intelligent and not a coward: that is a reconciliation which will permit me to see you from time to time. I swear to you on the head of my son, who for me is *everything*, that no evil thought crosses my mind. No – but I loved you too much and suffer so much that I ask this as a final plea.

I will be very strong. You know my present situation; materially I lack for nothing, mostly earning my own living.

My health is very bad, the pulmonary tuberculosis is sadly doing its work . . . Some good moments – some bad –

But I can't go on any longer – I would just like a little less hatred from you. I beg you to think well of me. Console me a little. I am too unhappy and I ask for a little bit of affection that would do me so much good.

I swear to you that I have no ulterior motives.

I have for you all the tenderness that I must have for you.

She signed it formally: 'Simone Thiroux'. At this time her son Gérard was two years and seven months old. He'd been christened Serge Gérard. Madame Diriks was his godmother and André Delhay, a parliamentary journalist, his godfather. The christening party had been given by Madame Diriks on the first floor of the Closerie des Lilas on the same day as Jeanne gave birth to little Jeanne in Nice.

Jeanne went to church and prayed, then saw her parents. Her mother, looking at her, said, 'It's all I expected, only worse.' She could not in the circumstances wish her a customary Happy New Year. Jeanne was too proud to admit anything. They weren't right, neither was she, but she kept her pain to herself and left.

The more of a failure Modigliani felt himself to be, the more of a show-off he became in public. His sarcasm, an ever-ready blade, caused fights and could end in a prison cell. If he didn't get home by a certain hour, usually over Ortiz de Zárate's shoulders, she'd go into the night to find him. If he was at a bar she'd try and persuade him out of it. This could arouse violence. If he was in the police station she'd get him out and bring him home.

Chana Orloff described Jeanne very pregnant, sitting on a bench near the Rotonde. She confided in Chana that things were not well. Chana said, 'Jeanne had to get him from the police station every night.'

On New Year's Eve he took a wild dive into oblivion. Paulette Jourdain remembers him turning up at the Zborowskis' with a huge bunch of flowers, so drunk he could hardly stand. It was seven in the morning. She was amazed someone so ill could have such stamina. They tried to get him to bed.

Modigliani blamed Paris, fate, then Zborowski. He turned on him as he once had on Kisling, accusing him of speculating on his work. Zborowski had had enough. Other rows followed. The quarrel became final. Jeanne took Modigliani's side. From now on they were on their own.

Indenbaum saw him just before he died. He said that Modigliani was unrecognisable. He had lost his voice and spoke strangely. He said he was leaving for Italy. He needed sun. It was too grey in Paris. Indenbaum said he died in complete destitution, whatever people said afterwards. No one looked after him any more. '*Zborowski n'était plus là* . . .' Zborowski was no longer there. Indenbaum said that people who called themselves his true friends turned away when they saw him. 'The world did not want Modi and Modi was too much for the world of his time.' Salmon said the same: Modigliani died in abject poverty.

He managed to put a few final touches to the portrait of his last sitter, Mario Varvogli, the Greek musician. The paint was still wet on the canvas when he went out for the last time. It was a bitterly cold January night. Jeanne was frightened and said she'd go with him. He went without her or a coat. He'd be gone for five minutes. He was gone hours. He showed up in the Rotonde, 'very drunk, his eyes – wild and ... in one of his worst cantankerous moods, quarrelsome, abusive and terribly emaciated'. Some artists, including Vicomte de Lascano Tegui, were going across town to see a draughtsman, Benito, near the rue d'Alésia. This was a long way from the Rotonde but Modigliani, despite their pleas to the contrary, insisted on accompanying them. It was clear to them all that he was a very sick man, wild and hallucinating, shouting abuse, 'attracting the attentions of passers-by, as it was already late, to another drunken, mad artist'. The rain drenched him, a coat was 'trailing behind him like the skin of a slain animal'. He followed the artists at some distance. Lascano dropped back '. . . and tried to reason with Modi, but only met with abuse'. When he reached the Lion of Belfort monument he saw it as 'some dreadful monster, for he yelled insults and challenges at it'.

He refused to go into Benito's house, or home to Jeanne. When the artists left the house, some time later, he was still standing in the cold and rain. Lascano said, 'He wanted to "get" everybody. He had no friends; never had had any; they were all traitors, mountebanks and far worse. He wanted them all to sit in the cold on a seat on the boulevard, raving that it was the quay of some imaginary miraculous sea. Nothing would shift him.'

Struggling and shouting, he then sat in the doorway of a church on the rue d' Alésia, 'where before his feverish eyes passed wild visions of Soutine, sombre streets of Utrillo, fantastic policemen in white gloves and blue capes coming to arrest him'. A prostitute tried to placate and comfort him. He started 'babbling to her about a phantom boat'. He collapsed and was taken back to Jeanne.

He had lost his friends, had nobody to rely on. This bears out what Indenbaum said about Zborowski not being there. But Jeanne was there and wondered how five healthy men could not have put one sick man into a taxi hours ago and got him home.

She put him to bed; the next day he was delirious. She hurried down to Ortiz. He was away. There were lower flats full of Modigliani enemies. She went down the four flights of stairs, across the courtyard into the first building and on to the street. She got the barman at the Rotonde to send for a doctor and Zborowski.

The doctor came. Zborowski, apparently in retrospect, had flu. The doctor gave Modigliani medicine and told him to stay in bed. It was nephritis, a kidney infection. He'd had it before and it had passed. Jeanne tried to give him hot water. He wanted alcohol. She wanted to summon his brother. He wouldn't hear of it. She said again that they could get him back to Italy. Too late! He wanted to leave in another direction – the Rotonde. But his body had finally given in. He was dying. She was about to give birth. She could see the irony. She still had choice. It had to be her alone, or her and him. She fused with him, gave him her energy so he could work. He finished the last touches to the Mario picture with a sure hand, then fell back on the bed. Bitterly he said, 'Another painting you couldn't even give away. Why should I fill up the world with what they don't want?' He didn't want to die, just as he didn't want to live. He spat blood, refused another doctor, wouldn't have one near him. He still expected to get up. He always had. Then he lay in her arms and she warmed him as he used to warm her. He asked her not to leave him. He slept restlessly.

The next day he was worse and she said she was going to get help. His body might have been finished, but energy still coursed through it. He shouted at her. He raged. She was reduced to silence – once silent around enemies, now silent around herself. There was nothing to eat except sardines, nothing to drink except alcohol. She opened a tin. He asked for alcohol. She waited for people to come. It was now the third day.

No one came on the fourth either. She drew ways of dying because now all she had to decide was her manner of death. It was the only choice left her. He lay feverish, occasionally muttering incoherently. There was no more coal and the room was freezing. She considered going down the stairs for help, saw herself curving around flight

129

after flight, across the icy courtyard. She didn't have the strength even to finish the journey in her imagination.

On the fifth day she felt very panicked. She was standing staring at the wall. She was too frightened to scream or speak or move. The thoughts arising inside her head were too unbearable, purgatorial . . . Quite calmly he spoke. He told her to come and sit by him. His voice was almost gone. He pointed to a piece of New Year wrapping string. It was gold, shining amongst the jumble of the studio.

She gave it to him and, smiling, he put her hands together and tied them at the wrists. Then he put his hands with hers and tied his wrists. Then he wound the gold string around both sets of bound wrists so that their four hands were joined together. It wasn't a tight knot, because he was too weak. He promised her they would be together always, and eternity was considerably preferable to Paris. She promised she'd be with him, as she always had.

Then he slept and she pulled off the loose cord and drew a design. The joined wrists. She wrote, 'our hands bound together in gold, linked for ever'. She wrote a letter, not to Bibi any more, but to the friend she wished she had and needed. She thought of the steely sea in Brittany, and how she'd despised herself for her obsessions. How she felt no good. And how her prayer would be to go to an unknown destination. It no longer seemed likely to be an earthly one.

She sat beside him, then lay beside him on the bed stained with sardine oil. The terrible pain in his head had started. His neck was stiffening. Time was no longer important to her. She'd lost time. They lay close together, mute, sensing the end.

Chapter Seventeen

On the seventh day Ortiz found them and called an ambulance. Jeanne didn't want Modigliani to be taken from her. She knew he was dying. She wanted at least to have him to herself for that short time. There was nothing the doctors could do. But as usual, there was someone taking him away.

Modigliani spoke his last words to Ortiz. As he was carried out he came to and said, 'I have kissed my wife goodbye. We are assured of eternal happiness.'

Hedwige brought Jeanne hot broth and stayed with her until Hanka arrived. She was too weak to be moved. All day the women took it in turns to sit with her. They waited for news. Jeanne kept hold of the piece of gold cord. She didn't speak or move. She had a limp grip on life. Kisling sent a telegram to all the friends: 'It's all up with Modigliani'. For two days he was in great pain. Tubercular meningitis had set in. A weaker man would have died. Kisling, not Zborowski, made arrangements. Accounts do show that Zborowski and Hanka were at the hospital, but the letter Zborowski sent to Emanuele was the soothing kind sent to a relative: 'Everything was done. He was never alone.' That was disputed by several friends.

Modigliani still held on. On the third day, Friday, Jeanne asked to go to the hospital. She wanted to be with him. He'd slipped into a coma. She was taken to the Zborowskis' flat. Paulette Jourdain remembers her taking her hand and saying, 'Don't leave me.' But they did leave her. The Zborowskis put her into a hotel on the rue de Seine. Paulette took her there: 'She was so near her time she waddled like a duck.'

Jeanne spent the night alone in torment. Where were her friends now? No one to turn to, to comfort her. Coldly they'd put her somewhere unfamiliar, alone. She did not kill herself because she was not sure he was dead. The next day the chambermaid found a razor under her pillow. She was taken to see him. He was still unconscious. Ortiz said he'd been in great pain. They'd given him an injection.

Then Jeanne went to the Tarnier clinic, but they wouldn't admit her because she was not yet in labour.

Chana Orloff saw her leaving and said she was far too calm. She was taken to the Zborowskis'. They said she must go back to her parents. Germaine was brought in to try and persuade her. Jeanne didn't want to go back to the rue Amyot, to her father. They said it was the right thing. Where else could she go? What else could she do? On Saturday January the 24th, at 8.50 p.m., Modigliani died without regaining consciousness. Monsieur Hébuterne took Jeanne to the hospital. According to Stanislav Fumet, her father stayed at the door while she approached the body:

> She looked at it for a long time as if her eyes were living over her tragedy. She moved away walking backward to the door. When we reached her she was still holding on to the memory of the dead man's face and forcing herself not to see anything else.

Kisling said he could never forget her terrible cry at the sight of her dead lover: 'The most piercing cry that a woman uttered when confronted by the corpse of her man.' Kisling had seen men die in the trenches, 'but never had death seemed so frightful. Yet her face when she left the hospital was calm.'

Stanislav Fumet saw her walking with her father like a sleepwalker, heavily pregnant. She couldn't be alone. The clinic wouldn't admit her. The Zborowskis preferred her to go home to her family.

Artists' Quarter described Madame L (possibly Germaine) pleading with Jeanne:

> . . . to let them take her to the Tarnier clinic, where her room was reserved as her time was near. Only a few days before, proud and chaste, Jeanne Hébuterne had taken a friend's hand and placed it lightly on her belly, murmuring, 'Feel how it lives!'
>
> Poor blue-eyed Jeanne, so little given to speech and who so rarely laughed – perhaps she had an early premonition of her tragic end – was nearly insane with grief. As she was in no state to be left to sleep in the studio in the rue de la Grande Chaumière and would not go to the clinic, she was taken to the house of her parents . . . They were implored to look after her tenderly.

As always with Jeanne, the statements are conflicting, filtered through the awful veil of her death. Chana had already seen her trying to be admitted to the clinic.

Back in her old bedroom on the fifth floor at 8 rue Amyot, Jeanne could hear her parents and brother arguing, shouting. What was to be done with her? Not one but two illegitimate children. No money. His useless paintings. That's all he'd left, the monster who had seduced their daughter. All he could do was die like a dog. She could not stay with them – the disgrace! She lay on the bed hearing, seeing, but no longer truly alive. She knew what had to be done, had known for weeks. Indenbaum understood that: 'She knew Modi was dying because you could see him going. Her decision was not a rash impulse. For a long time she had stopped thinking. She knew what was going to happen to her all along.'

She was as good as dead that night in the hotel, the razor under her pillow. How could she save herself? She was already in purgatory.

André, according to Germaine Labaye, spent part of the night in her room. At four in the morning she went to the window and leapt out backwards, down to her death.

A workman found her body, carried it up the Hébuternes' flat. André would not accept it. He told the workman to take it where it belonged and gave the address of the studio in rue de la Grande Chaumière. The workman put it on a handcart and wheeled it through the winter streets. The *concierge* refused it entrance. The tenant Monsieur Modigliani no longer lived there. The workman took it to the police station and by order they sent it back to the studio, where it lay unattended for several hours.

In her autobiography, *Laughing Torso*, Nina Hamnett wrote of the funerals as they had been described to her:

On the day Modigliani died his cat jumped out of the studio window and was killed. Modigliani was given a fine funeral in Père Lachaise, and I believe an enormous crowd followed the hearse. His wife had always said that she would like to be buried in the same cemetery as he was. Her family would not allow this and she was buried in the Cimetière de Bagneux, where Oscar Wilde was originally buried. The friends of Modigliani and she went very early in the morning to the funeral and when the moment came when the funeral guests shake hands with the relations, they stood with their hands behind their backs as a protest.

Jeanne's friend Chantal Quenneville wrote to the orphaned daughter to try and clarify some of the mystery and confusion surrounding the death. Jeanne Modigliani included her account in her biography, *Modigliani sans légende*:

Jeanne Hébuterne had sought refuge with her parents, Catholics offended by her union with the Jewish Modigliani, and did not say a word.

Two or three days had slipped by when I asked André Delhay: What about Jeannette? He gave me a black look. She had thrown herself out the fifth-floor window of her parents' home. The broken body had been picked up in the courtyard by a workman, who had carried it to the fifth-floor landing, where the horrified parents slammed the door in his face. The same workman had then brought the body over to the Grande Chaumière studio in a cart. Here the *concierge* refused to accept it saying 'it was not that of a tenant'. Finally this workman, who remained unknown and merited being decorated, went to the police station, where he was told to bring it back to the rue de la Grande Chaumière on orders of the police. There the body stayed, neglected the whole morning long.

Jeannette Léger was with me. We went to the studio right away; the sight of the body of this young woman, so gifted, so devoted in her love for Modigliani, gave us great pain. She had been my friend at the École des Arts Décoratifs and the Académie Colarossi. Jeanne Léger went to look for a hospital attendant to dress the body. I stayed alone at the harrowing scene. The head, white and sprinkled with spots of green, still bore traces of that life which she had renounced of her own heroic free choice. She had a child by Modigliani and was expecting another. Her belly jutted out under the coarse blanket. One leg seemed to have been broken in the fall . . .

I put things in order a little, swept the studio, which was full of empty boxes of preserves and coal. In the other room, just about everywhere, there were bottles of wine, also empty. On the easel there was a fine portrait of a man, which was not finished. I saw drawings by Jeanne in which she had portrayed herself, just as she looked with her long braids, in the act of stabbing herself in the breast with a long knife. Had she foreseen her own end?

Modigliani's funeral services were impressive. All Paris came to Père Lachaise. There were so many flowers. The war was over; we didn't want to look sad and we were used to death.

Jeanne's burial was far different from that of the man she had so humbly adored. Her parents didn't want to see anybody. They planned to put her into the ground at eight o'clock in the morning. Somebody managed to learn the details. Who was there to represent us at this unlikely hour? Zborowski, Kisling, André Salmon and their wives were in one taxi. In another were the parents, the brother, Chana and I. The pitiful hearse and the two taxis made the interminable trip out to one of those dismal cemeteries in the distant suburbs under cold grey skies.

Again the facts are not remembered clearly. It is as though Jeanne defies capture in time. Certainly two or three days didn't go by, because she took her life the morning after he died. It seems strange to learn casually of the death and rush to the studio, where there was no one in attendance. Jeanne's body fell directly down into the street, not into the courtyard, which is opposite and would have required quite an athletic jump from the window. Jeanne went backwards and landed below. But there does seem to have been confusion about how long the body remained alone, and how many hours it remained in the studio before burial. Two friends of Modigliani's kept watch over the body all night to deter rats. Georges Charaire said the Jeanne and Modigliani story was odd because no one really knew what happened, 'yet they know things, every detail about something that happened in the area a hundred years ago. But about Modigliani – ' he shrugged. 'I remember Ortiz de Zárate very well. But he never said a thing about Modigliani's death.'

The crowds of friends at Modigliani's funeral! Yet as she lay with him as he was dying there didn't seem to be one.

Roger Wild wrote to André Salmon, trying to define what Modigliani had felt for this girl: 'Jeanne adored him and he, who did not respect much, had a pure and very tender love for her, full of delicacy. But into her family, who detested him, he brought, as he always did – drama.'

Yet the Zborowskis had left alone in a hotel this person who had been so precious to Modigliani. They'd sent her back to her parents. With Kisling they concerned themselves with the paintings and the majestic funeral.

Marie Wassilieff covered Jeanne with some magnificent Russian sheets. Hanka, seeing her on the low stained bed, said she looked prettier in death than she ever had in life.

Death allowed Modigliani to be recognised. Everything he'd ever wanted in life – the acclaim, even the money – rushed his way the moment he was in his grave. Instantly he was a legend. Jeanne's dying enhanced it. They said he had genius. The Montparnasse friends and acquaintances were busy rewriting their versions of his last days. Jeanne's family and her childhood friends remained silent. They held the tragedy to themselves, as though they did not intend to lose or tarnish one drop of their anguish by sharing it with strangers. The women who'd loved him told their story. So did his drinking companions.

How unlikely that this quietly brought up girl from an ordinary Catholic family would be the love of Modigliani's life! But her very way of being prepared her for that passion. Those virtues, instilled in her from an early age by the Hébuternes – the practice of devotion, patience, purity, which they believed would protect her and prepare her for marriage to the proper man – fitted the doomed artist like a glove. The Modigliani who belonged to the fourteenth-century Italian masters also belonged to her. Her strength and gentleness, sudden gaiety and loyalty, even her resistance to her background, her warmth, made her his love.

Jeanne and Modigliani had chosen to be together. She was his true friend. Their enemies were religion, convention and disease.

Perhaps, as those who were there at the end said, he wanted Jeanne to join him. They weren't intended to be apart. He did not want her to suffer. Theirs just weren't the ideal circumstances for love.

Finale

Most of Modigliani's women met a tragic end. They had that, and him, in common. In October 1943 his first mistress, Beatrice Hastings, was found dead at her home in Worthing, England. She'd gassed herself. The coroner said, 'Suicide while mentally unhinged'. She was in her mid sixties.

In 1921 Simone Thiroux died of tuberculosis. Her son Gérard was adopted by a couple whose identity remained secret. Modigliani was the love of her life, and his rejection drained her will to go on living. She went to see him on his deathbed at the Charity hospital and walked in his funeral procession 'almost unnoticed in the crowd, a tall pallid girl . . . sad, silent'.

She continued to live in the same building as Dr and Madame Diriks, and tried to support herself by working as assistant nurse at the Cochin hospital. But she didn't have the strength for the job. She never held Modigliani's treatment of her against him, although many of her friends detested him for his callousness. She neglected her health until the day she died. Madame Diriks tried to persuade her to rest in bed, but there she sat on the Rotonde terrace.

In *Artists' Quarter* Madame Diriks wrote:

I was so angry that I pretended I hadn't seen her, but she ran after me, making all sorts of excuses and saying that she had only come out to get some air for half an hour.

'You must be crazy sitting out there in midwinter. And I told you you were not to get up – let alone go out. Now will you obey me or will you not? If you won't I shall never have anything to do with you again.

But Simone couldn't take even recriminations seriously. Madame Diriks continued:

[she] laughed gaily and coughed. I noticed with horror that the handkerchief that she had put to her mouth was bloodstained. Again she failed to keep her word. Instead of going to bed she went after dinner to dance at the Café Versailles. Later in the evening she had a severe haemorrhage and was rushed to the Cochin hospital. There, shortly afterwards, she died.

After their unhappy parting in autumn 1919, Lunia never saw Modigliani again. She wrote of her return to Paris in *Recollections of Lunia Czechowska*. The reactions of her friends seemed surprisingly odd:

I returned to Paris in September 1920 and went to the Zborowskis. I asked for news of Modigliani and they told me he was in Livorno but too ill to paint any more. All the friends that I remet said the same thing. I spent the first night in a room where Modigliani produced many of his great works. I had a strange dream. I was in Bourbon Archambault and I had gone to the small park on a plateau which dominates the thermal spa. It was autumn and everything was covered with chestnut leaves. There wasn't a person around. Alone with Modigliani I leaned against the park railing. He held something which looked like a magazine. He opened it and told me, 'Look, Lunia. Here it says I'm dead. Don't you find that a bit strong? You can see I'm not dead. You yourself can see!' At that moment I caught sight of Jeanne Hébuterne, who came towards us down below in the street. I said to him, there's Jeanne. Call her. He restrained me. 'No no. In an instant.' But duty towards Jeanne, who was looking for him, made me call out and I woke up.

The next day she challenged the Zborowskis, who said they'd been trying to spare her pain. Another interpretation she gave Fifield was that they did not want her to know they'd sold his paintings of her and didn't want to have to account for them.

And the daughter, Jeanne Modigliani, had an unhappy end. She died 'in drink'. Madame Schalit, Modigliani's niece, remembered his death – she was ten at the time.

Her parents came from Marseille and took little Jeanne from the nursery outside Paris: 'She was fourteen months and dressed from head to foot in black. My parents had never seen anything like it. But the nurse thought it was the right thing to do. After all, she was now an orphan. My parents took her to Paris and got new clothes, then brought her to Marseille.' Madame Schalit's voice was almost musical as she told me of her love for the child:

She was adorable, a superb baby. We kept her for six months or a year and wanted to go on keeping her. But Modigliani's sister Margherita, who was unmarried and childless, wanted to adopt her, which is strange because she did not like Modigliani, nor he her. It was through Emanuele, the Deputy, that the adoption was arranged. And Jeanne took the name Modigliani. Margherita was too strict, too hard with her. She was severe on the little girl. Jeanne studied and became a teacher. She met her husband Victor Nechtschein in Toulouse during the war. They were both involved in the Resistance. He went back to Paris, got divorced and married her. They had two daughters, girls, one unfortunately handicapped. I think that was what started her drinking. She taught at Lille University. Then she took up painting and had several exhibitions. But in the end she was unhappily alcoholic, lost her mind in alcohol. She died in 1984. She was sixty-six.

For a moment Madame Schalit looked sad.

They say people didn't want his paintings. How they regretted it afterwards – including my parents. What I could never understand was why, after he was dead, my mother and father went to the studio in the rue de la Grande Chaumière but did not take one painting. My father suggested my mother have one or two. There were canvases and drawings all over the floor. And she said, 'These horrors!' But she was provincial and she never did change her view of his work. There was a superb exhibition in 1958 in Paris and the Ambassador of Israel was there. He wanted to be introduced to Jeanne, the daughter, but she'd gone to a café and was too drunk. So my mother had to meet him instead. She, who didn't even like his paintings, had to listen to so much praise.

She returned again to the subject of the abandoned paintings. They were like an extension of the doomed couple: 'What the family could never understand was why his brother, the Deputy Emanuele, who was cultured and understood art, did not take a picture. He could have taken one as a souvenir for the little girl. There are many paintings I don't like or don't understand, but if I thought they'd be worth something . . .' She shrugged. 'Why didn't he see that? The family ended with nothing. The painter Derain gave the mother a portrait Modigliani had painted of him. There may have been one other, and a few drawings. Paulette Jourdain did give Jeanne her mother's work, out of respect. As a child, all Jeanne had was a piece of his velvet jacket that they gave her. It was made into a comforter.'

How often the family must have rehashed the facts, yet they never got them entirely right. Madame Schalit, under the impression that Modigliani tried to look after himself, said he had taken cures in Normandy. There is no confirmation of this. He did once join his Aunt Lo at Yport. She was worried by his deteriorating health and took a villa by the sea in 1911. He was supposed to go with her but found it difficult to leave Paris. She went on ahead, then sent him the money for the fare. She had to send it three times because he kept drinking it. After the third try he did get to the coast and arrived in an open carriage in a thunderstorm, wearing only a shirt. He was soaked to the skin because he'd taken the carriage to Fécamp to see the view.

The sight of him had upset Aunt Lo. He was tubercular and wild. How could she look after him? She returned him to Paris straight away. It didn't sound much like a health cure.

About Eugenia, Modigliani's mother, Madame Schalit said: 'She was a *grande dame*. Exceptional. She made a rich marriage but then her husband failed and she took over the family. She opened her school. She adored Dedo because he was the most fragile of her children. There wasn't a lot of money in the family but she always sent him an allowance to Paris. As soon as he got it he invited everyone to eat, to drink . . . and it was gone. She always wrote to him but had no idea he was in such a bad way.'

The Modiglianis accepted the fact that he drank – so did many of the artists and poets they admired. But they refused to accept that he was a drug addict. That did not fit in with something they could admire.

Madame Schalit did not find the last days in the studio mystifying, although many people she spoke to did. She thought Jeanne had gone 'a little crazy and lost her head. But they couldn't do anything for TB in those days. There were no antibiotics. There was no help. There was morphine for the pain in his head. That was all. Why not die in his own bed?'

Did the two families ever meet? The deaths seemed to divide them like an unhappy Romeo and Juliet, with the orphaned girl in the middle. Emanuele had continually tried to reason with the Hébuternes about reburying Jeanne. They also had a meeting after the death to discuss the adoption of the child. The Hébuternes had equal claim, but said they did not want her. They told Emanuele they could not understand why Jeanne chose that life.

Madame Schalit didn't find it surprising that the girl had taken her life with the baby so near to being born. She herself, the mother of five children and twenty-two grandchildren, was not lost for an answer: 'All the more reason to die. She already had one. How could she bring up two? Alone. She couldn't go through the bereavement. She followed him into death.'

She said it quite brightly, with no sadness. Life, even its tragedies, did not get her down.

Victor Nechtschein-Leduc, philosopher, said he met Jeanne during the Occupation when they were in the Resistance. He couldn't say that her parents dying in the manner they did had any effect on her because she hadn't known them. But then he is a philosopher.

Jeanne in fact spent several years of her life trying to find out what they were really like, the two people behind the legend. She found it difficult because the artists believed he belonged with them, had chosen to die with them and not with his family. And she, Jeanne, was considered family. Also they could tell her, the daughter whom they treated delicately, only selective things. Germaine Labaye was her best source, but when Jeanne went to see her in the sixties Germaine still found the suicide too terrible to talk about. She had never got over it and as her daughter said, she never did. And André Hébuterne consistently refused to see his sister's child. Jeanne couldn't understand 'why Uncle André continually refused to see me'. In the end, to try and resolve the mysteries, judge the evidence and strip the legends, she wrote her book. Jeanne was a physical part of those two people, inheriting both graces and less fortunate characteristics. Her drinking could have been hereditary, and her desire to paint.

Victor did have a lot to say about Modigliani's sister Margherita, who 'brought Jeanne up far too rigidly. She was too strict. It was not good for the child. She was maniacal. Also the Hébuternes had been too rigid in the manner in which they brought up their children.' Victor believed that was why André and Jeanne rebelled and went into the arts. This same rigidity and Catholicism, in his opinion, would not allow them to have their child's body brought into the house, which caused such a scandal: 'They had her poor corpse sent off with a stranger, unattended. The parents would not arrange the funeral. André had to do it. A bad affair.' Respect for Jeanne's death came in the end from the Modiglianis. Emanuele insisted on many occasions that she should be reinterred at Père Lachaise with Modigliani. At last, in 1929, Achille, her father, agreed and Jeanne was finally laid to rest.

Then he mentioned Gérard, Simone's child: 'Jeanne tried very hard to find him. She really wanted to see him.' And his eyes misted with tears. Poor Jeanne couldn't even find her half-brother. Her life seemed so cruel: 'We heard many rumours. Apparently he's a priest.'

Victor had two of his wife's pictures on a bedroom wall, along with a collection of Jeanne Hébuterne's drawings and a painting of a tree in the courtyard of the Grande Chaumière. There were line drawings by Modigliani. Then he showed Modigliani's family photograph album, a heart-shaped red book with a clasp. They looked graced, special. Finally he showed the photographs of Jeanne, his wife, at her last exhibition. Her eyes looked unfocused. He mentioned the sad effects of drink. Her final years had been terrible. He had found it necessary to divorce her in 1980. In 1984 she died. 'She drank until she finally lost her mind.'

Didn't he feel angry that Modigliani allowed himself to die and set going such a chain of tragedy? Surely his wife's early beginning, the loss of her parents, her subsequent upbringing by a woman who'd disliked her father, had provoked her terrible end – and not knowing, and being deprived of her father, so life-enhancing and charismatic, being cut off from him, hadn't that added to her problems? Wasn't Modigliani to blame?

Victor Nechtschein said simply, 'But he was a genius.' So that explained everything!

André Hébuterne did not have such a good life himself. He and the Hébuterne parents were reviled for their treatment of Jeanne. The blame, like the memory of the deaths, never receded. André chose to remain aloof. He continued to live and paint in the area that so disliked him. He had exhibitions of his landscapes but had little to do with the mainstream. The worst hell was having to watch the reputation of the man he had hated grow like a tree while he shrivelled in its shadow. He didn't challenge the terrible things that were written about him, but he couldn't still have been away when his sister died. How could he have instructed the handcart to be taken to the studio – and attended the funeral? This caused most people to find him guilty. Only Germaine Labaye stayed loyal.

Finally, in 1988, Georgette allowed a little of the truth about Jeanne to show. Perhaps too many of the people remaining had said too much, or perhaps it was hearing that little Jeanne had not had a wonderful upbringing in Italy, as André chose to believe. She'd died an alcoholic – that certainly took Georgette Hébuterne aback. Although they lived round the corner from Jeanne and Victor Nechtschein, the Hébuternes knew nothing about her death or circumstances. It was time to set the record straight.

Lina was born in Haut-de-Cagnes in 1919. She was the last of the 'Jacobellis'. After her, the mother had no more children. Emile Lejeune remembered them living in the ramshackle house opposite Le Pavillon des Trois Sœurs: 'They ran around like gypsies. They were poor Italians, barefoot. But Lina was different. Everyone in the village saw it immediately. She had *his* eyes.'

Other residents of Haut-de-Cagnes were in no doubt, Angelina said. Jacobelli's wife had fallen in love with the handsome Italian painter and that child she was carrying was his. Jacobelli, it seemed, didn't suspect, but after the birth people noticed that he knocked her about. He might have done so before, but the spotlight was not turned on him then. Angelina said Lina grew up the swan among the ugly ducklings. She didn't resemble the other children, her father, or even her mother. She was far too beautiful. And she had an elegance which didn't come from the farmer's family.

While recalling Lina, the residents of Haut-de-Cagnes remembered Père Curel. He was not an old trumpet-player, as described in biographies, but a respected doctor, involved, however, in the Mafia. There was a great deal of drug trafficking along the Riviera at that time. Angelina remembered that shortly after Modigliani left the coast, Curel had again lived in Le Pavillon des Trois Sœurs. One night there was a knock at the door; he opened it and was shot dead. That same night the pharmacist in the chemist's shop, still at the bottom of the steep hill today, was shot dead also. And one other – possibly a dentist. Curel, it seemed, was in some way connected with drug trafficking, and this was a revenge killing. Wherever Modigliani went, he never had far to look for what he wanted. In this case, the drugs were on his doorstep.

Louise Cornou has lived in Haut-de-Cagnes since 1938. She used to model for the great painters, including Matisse. She is a master chef specialising in Provençal cooking, and she has worked at some of the best hotels in the world. She looks as though she's come from the elements – strong, vibrant, beautiful, ageless. She adores the sun and knows how to enjoy life: 'When I first came here I noticed Lina. She was special. It wasn't just her beauty. She was inward and outward at the same time. She was then about nineteen. I can't remember what she did, but she certainly loved her mother. She was very very close to her. I never met Jacobelli. I think that was all over by then.'

Lina took Louise Cornou to an exhibition of Modigliani's paintings in Nice. She showed her 'more than one. Two, perhaps three, and said, "This is my mother".'

Angelina said the affair with Modigliani had gone on for months, and he came to visit Madame Jacobelli wherever he was staying. She posed for several pictures. By the time Lina was five she was undeniably like him. Now he was becoming famous. The villagers watched her grow, with a certain awe. Instead of 'troublesome drunk' he was now 'genius'. The paintings of Jacobelli's wife were worth thousands of francs.

Did Lina know he was her father?

Louise laughed, a rough cigarette laugh:

She sensed it. She never said it directly but then she wouldn't. She was a very private person. She let me know she knew, indirectly. And I respected that. She was 'knowing'. She knew things about life in a real sense. She was quite remarkable because she lived on two planes, in two worlds almost. She was very beautiful and dressed conservatively. Roger Lebon, the film director working at Victorine studios in Nice, fell in love with her. He was a lot older than her. They got married and lived in Paris. I used to visit them during the war. But Lina was always – sad. I think she longed for her father. She had a child, a boy, in Paris by Lebon. The child died, then Lebon died. The last time I saw Lina she was working in the Bon Marché store, in the perfume department.

Was Louise sure? Hadn't Monsieur Hébuterne worked there? A coincidence? Louise thought back, tried to remember. 'Maybe it was Printemps. But she sold perfume. That was just after the war. Then one night she went home. She lived near the Gare St Lazare. She shut the door and gassed herself.'

It seemed none of Modigliani's women came to a good end, except perhaps Lunia, who married a Baron Chorosco and ran a perfume shop behind Nice.

Did Lina know about Jeanne Hébuterne and her death? 'Absolutely,' said Louise. 'She was interested in all that because she took me to the exhibition of his work.'

Emile Lejeune's daughter-in-law, the painter Ulla Fribrock, has only recently discovered that her house, with its lovely feeling of calm and harmony, is Le Pavillon des Trois Sœurs. She had assumed that it no longer existed. She asked Angelina: where is it? Angelina said, 'You're living in it.' Ulla had heard stories about Lina and remembered the Jacobelli house, now renamed 'the house of Modigliani and Soutine'. Ulla had done a painting of it before the restoration. How run down it was! And all the children were ambitious; they all went away and did well – some to America. They all wanted to get as far away as they could from being poor. No one knew what had happened to Jacobelli's wife.

Jane Galsworthy, one of the descendants of John, remembers an Italian woman coming to visit her mother in Sloane Square in the fifties. The woman, Julietta, had been very beautiful, but was now a hunchback. She was lively and talked a lot about Modigliani. She'd been one of his great models, and also his mistress.

Mistress is a big word. None of his affairs with models was long-lived. At some point she'd married a titled person but now she had no money and was reduced to cleaning houses.

'My mother used to help her,' said Jane. 'She was very lively and obviously someone special. I remember that. And I could see how beautiful she'd been. She said the painter was the love of her life. She wasn't exaggerating because why would she bother to impress me, a child?'

Jacobelli's wife must have been born in the last years of the nineteenth century. She'd arrived in Haut-de-Cagnes in 1911 with Jacobelli and started having children. She'd had six before Modigliani appeared in 1918. If she was seventeen in 1911 she was born in 1894. Jane believed the Italian woman was certainly in her early sixties when she visited Sloane Square.

'It was the biggest thing in her life. Having loved Modigliani.'

Coda

When I felt compelled to write about Jeanne Hébuterne it seemed that there would be nothing more to find and that made me sad. The biographers said it was too late. Over Jeanne, a great silence. But I took the risk and set off on my journey. My search couldn't have been done sitting in an archive. I had to go back to those streets and neighbourhoods where her life ended and find those unwilling witnesses who still remained. And to the contrary, there was a great deal to be uncovered and resolved. So my journey was worth it.

Patrice Chaplin, London, 1990